A LITTLE GIANT® BOOK

JOKES

Joseph Rosenbloom

Illustrated by Sanford Hoffman

STERLING

New York / London
www.sterlingpublishing.com/kids

Library of Congress Cataloging-in-Publication Data

Rosenbloom, Joseph.
    Little giant book of jokes/ Joseph Rosenbloom; illustrated by Sanford
Hoffman.
      p. cm.
    Includes index.
    Summary: A collection of hundreds of jokes of all kinds, including one-liners,
  book and author lists, tongue twisters, and riddles.
  ISBN 1-8069-6101-5
  1. Wit and humor, Juvenile. 2. American wit and humor.
  [1. Jokes. 2. Riddles.] I. Hoffman, Sanford, ill. II. Title.
  PN6163.R57 1996
  818'.5402--dc20

                                                        96-28373
                                                          CIP
                                                          AC

Lot#: 10 9 8 7

03/12

Published by Sterling Publishing Co., Inc.
387 Park Avenue South, New York, NY 10016
Material in this book adapted from *Mad Scientist: Riddles, Jokes, Fun; School's
Out: Great Vacation Riddles & Jokes; Get Well Quick!* (published in paper as *Super
Sick Jokes & Riddles*); *Wacky Insults & Terrible Jokes; Wild West Riddles & Jokes,*
and *World's Best Sports Riddles & Jokes,* all © by Joseph Rosenbloom © 1996 by
Sterling Publishing Co., Inc.
Distributed in Canada by Sterling Publishing
c/o Canadian Manda Group, 165 Dufferin Street
Toronto, Ontario, Canada M6K 3H6
Distributed in the United Kingdom by GMC Distribution Services,
Castle Place, 166 High Street, Lewes, East Sussex, England BN7 1XU
Distributed in Australia by Capricorn Link (Australia) Pty. Ltd.
P.O. Box 704, Windsor, NSW 2756, Australia

Printed in China
Sterling ISBN-13: 978-1-4027-4973-5
        ISBN-10: 1-4027-4973-2

For information about custom editions, special sales, premium and
corporate purchases, please contact Sterling Special Sales
Department at 800-805-5489 or specialsales@sterlingpub.com.

CONTENTS

1. QUICKIES

TOURIST *(to farmer)*: Lived here all your life?
FARMER: Not yet.

Why did the cow jump over the moon?
The farmer had cold hands.

FIRST ROBOT: Do you have any brothers?
SECOND ROBOT: No, only transistors.

TOURIST: Can you give me a room and a bath?

DESK CLERK: I can give you a room, but you'll have to take your own bath.

FATHER: Bonnie, please take the dog out and give him some air.

BONNIE: Sure, Dad. Where is the nearest gas station?

HORACE: I lost my dog.

MORRIS: Why don't you put an ad in the paper?

HORACE: What good would that do? My dog can't read.

Did you ever see a wood fence?
No, but I saw the barn dance.

Did you hear about the dog that ate roasted garlic?
His bark was worse than his bite.

What is hard to beat?
A broken drum.

"Who do you think you're talking to?"
"How many guesses do I get?"

A thin man and a fat man ran a race. One ran in short bursts, the other ran in burst shorts.

DICK: I just flew in from Japan.
RICK: Boy, your arms must be tired.

EAGLE SCOUT: How can you tell a boy moose from a girl moose?
TENDERFOOT: By its moustache.

EAGLE SCOUT: What would you do if you found a sick bird?
TENDERFOOT: Give it first aid tweetment.

CITY VISITOR: How far can you push a chicken?
FARMER: Not far, but you can pullet.

GAME WARDEN: Have you ever hunted bear?

TOURIST: No, but I've gone fishing in my shorts.

HARRY: This match won't light.
LARRY: What's the matter with it?
HARRY: I don't know—it lit before.

NIT: How long can a person live without a brain?
WIT: How old are you?

FLIP: Do you have trouble making up your mind?
FLOP: Yes and no.

TED: What would you say if I told you that I had a bright idea?
NED: Nothing. I can't talk and laugh at the same time.

"Have you ever seen a line drive?"
"No, but I've seen a ball park."

DORIS: Look—there's a baby snake.
BORIS: How do you know it's a baby?
DORIS: You can tell by its rattle.

VICKIE: What does your mother do for a headache?
NICKIE: She sends me out to play.

"Mom, can I go out and play baseball?"
   "With those holes in your socks?"
"No, with the kids next door."

FATHER: If you kids don't stop making so much noise, I'll go deaf!
KID: Too late—we stopped an hour ago!

A lady telephoned the airline and asked how long it took to fly to Boston.
   The clerk replied, "Just a minute."
   "Thank you," said the lady, as she hung up.

TRAVELLER: I'd like a round trip ticket.
TICKET SELLER: I'm sorry—all our tickets are square.

TRAVELLER: I'd like a ticket to New York.
TICKET SELLER: Do you want to go by Buffalo?
TRAVELLER: Don't be silly. I want to go by plane.

JILL: How did you find the weather when you were on vacation?

BILL: I just went outside—and there it was!

DIP: Do you summer in the country?

PIP: No, I simmer in the city.

SIGN IN TRAVEL AGENCY WINDOW

PLEASE GO AWAY!

Did you hear about the latest invention?
It's a spinning top that is also a whistle.
Now you can really blow your top.

What is the difference between a tired old horse and a dead insect?

One is a seedy beast and the other is a bee deceased.

15

FIRST MOUSE: I finally got that scientist trained.

SECOND MOUSE: How so?

FIRST MOUSE: Every time I go through that maze and ring the bell, he gives me something to eat.

BUD: I just had my appendix removed.

DUD: Have a scar?

BUD: No, thanks, I don't smoke.

GLEN: I wish I were in your shoes.

JEN: Why would you want to be in my shoes?

GLEN: Because mine have holes in them.

MOTHER *(to sleeping son)*: Sidney, it's twenty to eight!

SIDNEY *(still sleepy)*: In whose favor?

"I've invented a computer that is almost human," said Dr. Frankenstein to Igor.

"You mean it can think?" asked Igor.

"No, but when it makes a mistake, it puts the blame on some other computer."

An apple a day keeps the doctor away–if it's aimed right.

"Excuse me, sir, but are you reading the newspaper you're sitting on?"

How do you catch baby frogs?
With a tadpole.

How do you make anti-freeze?
Put ice cubes in her bed.

AMBULANCE DRIVER: Have an accident?
VICTIM: No, thanks, I just had one.

2. WINNERS & LOSERS

SPORTS REPORTER: How do you feel about losing the race?
RUNNER: The agony of defeat.

Did you hear about the long-distance runner who took part in a 100-mile race? Well, he was in the lead and had one more mile to go, but he was too tired to finish, so he turned around and ran back.

WORLD'S SILLIEST MILKSHAKE JOKE

After ordering a milkshake, a man had to leave his seat in the restaurant to make a phone call. Since he didn't want anyone to take his drink, he took a paper napkin, wrote on it, "The world's strongest weightlifter," and left it under his glass.

When he returned from making his call, the glass was empty. Under it was a new napkin with new writing that said: "Thanks for the treat!" It was signed, "The World's Fastest Runner."

MINA: What is the best place to put crying children?
TINA: Where?
MINA: In the bawl (ball) park.

Harold came home from playing ball with tears streaming down his face. When his father asked him what was wrong, the little boy sobbed, "I was traded!"

"That shouldn't make you feel bad, Son. Even the greatest baseball players get traded."

"I know," replied Harold, "but I was traded for a torn glove."

COACH: Are you hurt?
FOOTBALL PLAYER *(moaning)*: I think so. Better call me a doctor.
COACH: Okay, you're a doctor.

CELESTE: Did you notice that I dropped some weight this summer?

PEST: From the look of your knees, you didn't drop it far enough.

The weightlifting champion was always bragging about his strength. Everybody was tired of listening to him boast. Finally a small man had an idea.

"I bet you," he said to the weightlifter, "that I can wheel something around the block in a wheelbarrow—but you can't wheel it back."

The weightlifter looked the small man up and down and said, "I'll take that bet."

The small man smiled, gripped the handles of the wheelbarrow, and said to the weightlifter, "Hop in, please."

He then wheeled the weightlifter around the block and won the bet.

JILL: Say, how did you break your finger?
BILL: Playing football in a telephone
  booth.
JILL: What?
BILL: I was trying to get my quarterback.

That weightlifter is so strong—

How strong is he?

He's so strong, he pitches horseshoes without taking them off the horses.

He's so strong that when he sticks out his tongue, he breaks a tooth.

Why did the sword swallower eat pins and needles?

He was on a diet.

24

On Jeffrey's birthday, his parents bought him what he always wanted—a horse. But the horse didn't seem to have any energy. Jeffrey took it to the vet.

"This horse is very old," the vet said, after looking him over.

"Will I be able to race him?" asked Jeffrey.

The vet looked at Jeffrey and then he looked at the horse. "Sure," he said, "and you'll probably win."

POLLY: I went riding today.
MOLLY: Horseback?
POLLY: Sure. It got back two hours before I did.

JANE: My horse wanted to go one way and I wanted to go the other.
RIDING INSTRUCTOR: What happened?
JANE: He tossed me for it.

CHICK: You play one-on-one basketball with your dog? He must be very unusual.

RICK: Not really. I beat him most of the time.

CARY: Did you hear about the runner who lost the marathon because of his socks?
GARY: No—how could that be?
CARY: They were guaranteed not to run.

LEN: If I arm-wrestled you, who would win?
GLEN: I give up—who?
LEN: I would. You just gave up.

COACH: We have a great team this year. So far we have had no losses, no draws and no goals scored against us.
REPORTER: How many games have you played?
COACH: The first one is next Sunday.

CUSTOMER: Do you sell football shoes?
CLERK: Sure. What size is your football?

GILLY: I know someone who is so dumb, he lost $20 betting on a football game.
DILLY: What's so dumb about that?
GILLY: Well, he lost $10 betting on the play—and the other $10 on the instant replay.

Melvin was playing football very badly. He tried to kick a goal and missed. Finally, he threw himself down on the bench and said in disgust, "Boy, I could kick myself."

The coach looked the other way.

"Don't bother," he said, "you'd probably miss."

Old football players never die—they just hang up their receivers.

How are football players like airline passengers?

Both want safe touchdowns.

DIZZY *(at concert)*: What's that book the conductor is looking at?

IZZY: That's the score.

DIZZY: Really? Who's winning?

TEACHER: Larry, why are you late for school?

LARRY: Well, teacher, I was dreaming about a football game, and it went into extra time—so I had to see the finish.

A veteran football coach saw his championship hopes fade when, with 10 seconds left in the game and his team behind by three points, a rookie player lost the ball. The other team picked it up and scored a touchdown.

"Well," said the coach sadly, "that's the way the rookie fumbles."

TONY: I'm no longer the quarterback on our team.

BONY: What happened.

TONY: It's all my mother's fault. She made me promise not to pass anything until somebody said, "Please."

BEST ANNOYING CUTE KID AT
FOOTBALL GAME JOKE

A man and his four-year-old son were watching a professional football game on TV. After a bad play, the father exploded:

"Just look at that stupid halfback! He fumbles three times, and every time the other team recovers! Why do they let someone like that play in the game?"

The little boy thought it over. "Daddy," he said, "maybe it's his ball."

That football player is so tough–

**How tough
is he?**

He's so tough, he parts his hair
with a chain saw.

He's so tough, he uses barbed wire
for dental floss.

He's so tough, he gargles with
Drano.

Did you hear about the big game hunter who took his rifle to the football game? He heard the Lions were playing the Bears.

REPORTER: What position do you play in
the football game?
PLAYER: Oh, sort of crouched down and
bent over.

What do you give a football player with
big feet?

Large shoes.

If athletes get athlete's foot, what do astronauts get?

Missile toe.

CAL: Do you know the difference between an old baseball glove and a piece of candy?

VAL: No.

CAL: Good. Then eat the old baseball glove and give me that piece of candy.

Dad was delighted to learn that his son had broken the school long-jump record.

"How did you do it, Son?" he asked.

"To tell the truth, Dad, I entered discus. But as I got ready to throw, I backed into a javelin."

Why did the athlete put on his right shoe first?

Because it would be stupid to put on the wrong shoe first.

Did you hear about the Olympic athlete
who jumped all over his Beatles album?
He was out to break a record.

DUFFY: When I was a sparring partner for
the heavyweight champion, I gave him
the biggest scare of his life.
MUFFY: You gave the champion a big
scare?
DUFFY: Yes—he thought he killed me.

WISE MAN SAYS:

Boxer who chews on foot
gets sock in mouth.

BOXER *(in his corner)*: Did I do him any
damage?
TRAINER: No, but keep on swinging. The
draft may give him a cold.

REFEREE: Now remember, at the bell, shake hands.

BOXER: I don't have to remember. Mine are shaking already.

MANAGER *(to fighter)*: Don't be afraid of him. Remember, if he were any good, he wouldn't be fighting you.

MANAGER *(to boxer)*: When I said to show him what you're made of, I didn't mean to let him knock the stuffing out of you.

What do prizefighters bring to a picnic? *A box lunch.*

Did you hear about the boxer who couldn't find anything to drink? Someone beat him to the punch.

What is a horse's favorite game?
  Stable tennis.

WORLD'S BEST CENTIPEDE JOKE

Some of the animals on Noah's ark decided to play baseball. One team was headed by an elephant, the other by a giraffe.

By the fourth inning, the score was 9-0 in favor of the elephant's team. In the fifth inning, a hard drive was stopped by a centipede in a neat catch.

"What a great catch!" said the giraffe to the centipede. "Where were you during the first four innings?"

The centipede answered, "I was putting on my sneakers."

THE BEST BASEBALL TALENT HUNT JOKE

A baseball scout found a remarkable prospect—a horse who was a pretty good fielder and who hit the ball every time he was up at bat. The scout got him a try-out with a big league team.

Up at bat, the horse slammed the ball into far left field and stood at the plate, watching it go.

"Run!" the manager screamed, "Run!"

"Are you kidding?" answered the horse. "If I could run, I'd be in the Kentucky Derby."

Little Arnold was pitching for the Little League team. After he walked the first six players that came up, he was taken out of the game.

"It isn't fair," he moaned. "I was pitching a no-hitter!"

FATHER: Son, you've struck out so many times with the bases loaded in the Little League playoffs, I might have to do something I don't want to do.
JUNIOR: What's that, Dad?
FATHER: I may have to trade you.

Did you hear about the baseball player who was so kind, he wouldn't even hit a fly?

DO-IT-YOURSELF HEALTH
BOOKS

1. *Sports Injuries*
by Charlie Hawes & Aiken Bakke

2. *Curing Poison Ivy*
by Donna S. Crachit

3. *Successful Dieting*
by Yukon Dewitt & Troy Hodder

4. *Do You Need Surgery?*
by Noah I.L. Waite

How did the cow feel when it struck out
every time it came to bat?
Like an udder failure.

FATHER: I hear you played hookey from
school today to play baseball.
SON: No, Dad, and I have the fish to
prove it.

"I don't know what's the matter with me today," said the baseball player as he struck out several times in a row. "I'm not playing my usual game."

"Oh?" said the coach sarcastically. "What game is that?"

JAN: Will you join me in a game of tennis?
DAN: Why? Are you coming apart?

PATIENT: Doctor, I've been fighting and fighting this cold and it won't go away.
DOCTOR: There's your mistake. Never fight a cold. That's what makes a cold sore.

PATIENT: Will you give me something for my cold?
DOCTOR: Why should I? I already have a cold.

Why did the grown-up cows worry about
the little cow?

Because it was so moo-dy.

Why did the big bucket worry about the
little bucket?

It was a little pail (pale).

Did you hear about the baseball game between the "Collars" and the "Shirts"? The game ended in a tie.

"I have some good news and some bad news," said the doctor. "First for the good news. You're very sick and have only 24 hours to live."

"You call that good news?" sobbed the patient. "I have only 24 hours to live? What could be worse than that?"

"Now for the bad news," said the doctor. "I should have told you yesterday."

My uncle had so many operations that when they removed the stitches, he fell apart.

3. SPACE-Y

MOTHER: I think Junior is going to be an astronaut.

FATHER: What makes you think so?

MOTHER: I spoke to his teacher today, and she said all he's good for is taking up space.

ASTRONAUT: Wanna fly?

COPILOT: Sure.

ASTRONAUT: Wait a second—I'll catch one for you.

What do you call a spaceman who is invisible?

An astro-naught.

What do you call a crazy spaceman?

An astro-nut.

Two astronauts were in a space craft circling thousands of miles above the earth. According to plan, one astronaut was to leave the ship and go on a 15-minute space walk. The other was to remain inside.

After completing his walk, the first astronaut tried to get back inside, but the door was locked. He knocked. There was no answer. He knocked louder. Still no answer. He pounded with all his might.

Finally, after what seemed like hours, a voice from inside the space craft spoke up: "Who's there?"

Two men from Mars, the first to land on Earth, stepped out of their spaceship near a large town. Pointing to the TV aerials on almost every house, one happily said to the other, "Look—girls!"

"What do you say when a Martian walks up to you with a death-ray gun?"

"I give up."

"That's right! Only you say it faster."

Two Martians landed on a corner with a traffic light.

"I saw her first," one Martian said.

"So what?" said the other, "I'm the one she winked at."

"What's the difference between a Martian and a snoo?"

"What's snoo?"

"Nothing much. What's snoo with you?"

"What's the difference between a Martian and a pottfer?"

"What's a pottfer?"

"It's to cook in, silly."

SAY THESE 3 TIMES QUICKLY

Seth's sharp spacesuit shrank.

The spaceship's back brake-block broke.

"Sure, the spaceship's ship-shape, sir!"

Two Martians landed in the Atlantic Ocean. One said, "Hey, man, look at all that water."

The second Martian thought for a moment and said, "Yeah, and that's only the top."

Two businessmen met on the street.

"Sam," said one, "have I got a bargain for you! I can get you a full-grown Martian for $50!"

"How big is this Martian?" Sam asked, trying to hide his interest.

"He's 10 feet tall and weighs 5 tons."

"Are you nuts?" Sam said. "You know I live in a tiny apartment with my wife and 4 children. What do I want with a 10-foot tall Martian who weighs 5 tons?"

"You drive a hard bargain. How about two Martians for $75?"

Sam smiled. "Now you're talking!" he said.

MARTIAN: Are you tan from the sun?
ASTRONAUT: No, I'm Sam from the Earth.

How did Mary's little lamb get to Mars?
By rocket sheep.

What do Martian chickens lay?
Eggs-terrestrials.

What is better than presence of mind
when a Martian aims a death-ray at you?
Absence of body.

BEST SELLER LIST

How to Use Space Weapons
by Ray Gunn

How to Find UFOs
by Luke Sharpe

Space Invaders Are Here
by Athena Landon

Is There Intelligent Life in Space?
by Y. Knott

Living on the Moon
by Yul B. Sari

ASTRONAUT #1: Forget the moon—
everybody is going to the moon. We'll
go directly to the sun.

ASTRONAUT #2: We can't go to the sun. If
we got within 13 million miles of it, we'd
melt.

ASTRONAUT #1: Okay, so we go at night.

"I see your new telescope only magnifies
three times."

"Oh, no! I've used it twice already!"

4. WILD WEST

Did you hear about the cowboy who was trampled by a flock of sheep? He dyed-in-the-wool.

What 7 letters of the alphabet did the outlaw say when he opened the bank vault and found nothing inside?

O I C U R M T.

Why did the cowboy aim his gun at the fan?

He was just shooting the breeze.

DOCTOR: Ever have an accident?

COWBOY: No.

DOCTOR: Never in your whole life?

COWBOY: Well, on the last roundup, a bull charged and broke three of my ribs.

DOCTOR: Don't you call that an accident?

COWBOY: No, Doctor, the bull did it on purpose.

A rancher walked up to the window at the post office, where a new clerk was sorting mail.

"Any mail for Mike Howe?" the rancher asked.

The clerk ignored him and the rancher repeated his question in a louder voice. Without looking up, the clerk said, "No, none for your cow, and none for your horse, either."

Why did the cowboy carry a cannon into town?

He wanted people to think he was a big shot.

Why did the cowboy ignore the "Danger" sign on the cliff?

Because he thought it was only a bluff.

Did you hear the story about the branding iron? It's too hot to handle.

Why did the cowboy put his bunk in the fireplace?
So he could sleep like a log.

"Sheep are the stupidest creatures."
"What did you say, my lamb?"

A cowboy was leading a flock of sheep down Main Street when the Sheriff ordered him to stop.

"What's wrong?" the cowboy asked. "I was just heading my ewes into a side street."

"That's the trouble," the Sheriff replied. "No ewe turns are permitted in this town."

What happened when the horse swallowed a dollar?

It bucked.

What would you have if Batman and Robin were run over by stampeding cattle?

Flatman and Ribbon.

What newspaper do cattle read?
  The Daily Moos.

What is the best way to count cows?
  With a cow-culator.

BESTSELLERS IN THE DUDE
RANCH LIBRARY

Bareback Riding
by Eiffel Downe & Lord Howard Hertz

How to Identify Cattle
by Brandon Irons

Breaking Wild Horses
by Aiken Bach & Yul B. Sorry

My Life as a Cowgirl
by Rhoda Haas

Lawmen at Work
by Hans Zupp

What sickness do cowboys get from riding
wild horses?
  Bronchitis.

What happened after the cowboy drank
eight Cokes?
He burped 7-Up.

BESTSELLERS IN THE DUDE
RANCH LIBRARY

Protect Your Ranch
by Bob Dwyer

Cowboy Yodelling
by O. Leo Layee

Donkeys in the West
by Jack Cass

My Life as an Outlaw
by I. Ben Bad

SHERIFF: There's a man in the circus who jumps on a horse's back, slips underneath, catches hold of his tail, and finishes on the horse's neck.

TENDERFOOT: That's nothing. I did all those things the first time I rode a horse.

DEPUTY: Ouch! My new boots hurt when I walk in them.

SHERIFF: No wonder! You have them on the wrong feet.

DEPUTY: But I don't have any other feet!

As the Lone Ranger and Tonto were riding along towards the north, they spotted a war party of about 50 Apaches coming at them. They turned south, but another war party appeared. Concerned now, the Lone Ranger and Tonto turned east and met another war party of 100 braves. They turned west as their last remaining hope and saw a war party of 500.

The Lone Ranger turned to his friend and said, "Well, Tonto, this is the end. I guess we're goners."

Tonto looked back at the Lone Ranger. "What do you mean *we*, paleface?"

FIRST TENDERFOOT: Can you ride a horse?
SECOND TENDERFOOT: Don't know.
    Couldn't stay on one long enough to find out.

What kind of fur do you get from a bull?
As fur as you can get.

DEPUTY: I hear that a charging bull won't
hurt you if you carry a flashlight.
SHERIFF: True—if you carry it fast enough.

The cowboy strode into the restaurant
yelling, "All right, all right, who is the wise
guy who painted my horse yellow?"

There was silence in the restaurant.

"Show yourself, if you dare!" shouted
the cowboy.

A 7-foot-tall, mean-looking character got
up from a table and rested his hands on
his gun handles. "I did it," he said coolly.
"What did you want to tell me?"

The cowboy swallowed hard. "I thought
you'd like to know," he said, "the first coat
is dry."

RANCHER: You want to work around here?
  Can you shoe horses?
COWHAND: No, but I can shoo flies.

BIFF: What's the name of your ranch?

CLIFF: The ABCDEFGHIJKLMNOPQRS
TUVWXYZ Ranch.

BIFF: How many head of cattle do you
have?

CLIFF: Not many.

BIFF: How come?

CLIFF: Not many survive the branding.

A cowboy visited a saloon where he saw a
remarkable sight. Several cowboys were
sitting around a table playing poker with a
small, shaggy dog.

"What a wonderful dog," the cowboy
said. "He must be very intelligent to be
able to play poker with human beings."

"Not really," one of the players said.
"Every time he gets a good hand, he wags
his tail."

An old prospector marched into an
assayer's office and threw two huge
nuggets on the counter. The clerk stared at
them, open-mouthed.

"Well," said the prospector impatiently,
"don't just stand there! Assay something!"

SAY THESE 3 TIMES QUICKLY

The Sheriff shot a shy thrush.

Six sheriffs seek six sick sheiks.

Six cattle slip on slick ski slopes.

COWBOY *(boasting)*: Out on the range I can
    live for a week on a can of sardines.
CITY MAN: How do you keep from falling
    off?

How do you treat an outlaw with an itchy
trigger finger?
   With respect.

What do you call an outlaw with cotton stuffed in his ears?

Anything you want. He can't hear you.

A cowboy rides a horse from Dodge City to Abilene. The trip normally takes four days. He leaves Dodge City on Wednesday and arrives on the same Wednesday. How can this be?

His horse is named Wednesday.

TENDERFOOT: How do you lead a wild stallion?

COWBOY: It's simple. First you get a rope. Then you tie it to the wild stallion.

TENDERFOOT: And then?

COWBOY: And then you find out where the wild stallion wants to go.

5. DOCTOR, DOCTOR!

DOCTOR: Nurse, did you take the patient's temperature?

NURSE: Why, no, Doctor. Is it missing?

NURSE: Shall we give the patient a local anesthetic, Doctor?

DOCTOR: No, I'm in a hurry. Let's give him the express.

PATIENT: Doctor, what do you think of artificial respiration?
DOCTOR: Personally, I prefer the real thing.

TEACHER: How did you get that lump on your head?
JOSE: I got hit by some beans.
TEACHER: How could some little beans give you such a big lump?
JOSE: They were still in the can.

PATIENT: Doctor, what's the difference between ammonia and pneumonia?
DOCTOR: Ammonia comes in bottles; pneumonia comes in chests.

DOCTOR: The operation will cost you $400.
PATIENT: Can't you do it for $200?
DOCTOR: Sure. But for $200, I use duller knives.

A man went to his doctor, complaining about terrible neck pains, throbbing headaches, and dizzy spells. The doctor examined him and said, "I regret to inform you that you have only six months to live."

The doomed man decided he would spend the time he had left enjoying himself.

He took all his money out of the bank and bought a car, a boat and a plane. Then he went to get himself fancy clothes. First he went in to buy something he always wanted: a dozen custom-made shirts.

The tailor measured him and said, "You have a size 17 neck."

"No, you're wrong," said the man. "I wear a size 15 neck and that's what I want."

"I'd be glad to do it for you, sir," the

tailor said. "But if you wear a size 15 neck, you'll probably have terrible neck pains, throbbing headaches, and dizzy spells."

DOCTOR, DOCTOR!

PATIENT: Doctor, doctor, I have a hoarse throat.

DOCTOR: Believe me, the resemblance doesn't end there.

PATIENT: Doctor, doctor, I feel like a cup of coffee.

DOCTOR: Oh, perk up and don't be a drip.

MOTHER: Doctor, doctor, my little boy has swallowed a bullet!

DOCTOR: Well, don't point him at anybody.

DOCTOR: Breathe out three times.
PATIENT: So you can check my lungs?
DOCTOR: No, so I can clean my eyeglasses.

REPORTER: Doctor, what is the best way to prevent diseases caused by biting insects?
DOCTOR: Don't bite any.

PATIENT: Doctor, doctor, my stomach hurts!
DOCTOR: Stop bellyaching!

REPORTER: Doctor, what is your favorite sport?
DOCTOR: Sleighing.
REPORTER: Well, er, I meant, aside from business.

"Martin went to Arizona for his asthma."
   "What's the matter? Couldn't he get it here?"

"Doc, give it to me straight—what kind of shape am I in?"

"Let's put it this way. From now on you pay in advance."

DOCTOR: I want to take out your appendix this evening.

PATIENT: That's okay with me, but please bring it home early.

PATIENT: Will you treat me?

DOCTOR: Absolutely not! You'll have to pay like everyone else.

DOCTOR: How are you doing with that new patient?

NURSE: He's a nuisance. Yesterday he cried all day because he lost four teeth.

DOCTOR: What's wrong with that? I'd be pretty upset if I lost four teeth.

NURSE: From his comb?

PATIENT: I snore so loud, Doctor, I can't fall asleep. What should I do?

DOCTOR: Sleep in the next room.

What's the difference between a cow with
a sore throat and an angry crowd?
One moos badly, the other boos madly.

NURSE, NURSE!

PATIENT: Nurse, nurse, I swallowed a spoon!
NURSE: Well, lie down and don't stir.

PATIENT: Nurse, nurse, I swallowed a roll of film!
NURSE: Don't worry–nothing serious will develop.

PATIENT: Nurse, nurse, I was playing my harmonica and I swallowed it!
NURSE: Lucky you weren't playing a piano!

WITCH DOCTOR *(to sick native)*: Drink this potion of ground bat wing, lizard tail, alligator scale and hawk feathers.

SICK NATIVE: I drank that yesterday and it didn't work.

WITCH DOCTOR: Okay, take two aspirins and call me in the morning.

DARRYL: I went to a doctor and he told me that my liver is 10 inches long.
CAROL: Well, that shows you come from a line of long livers.

DOCTOR: Sorry I made you wait so long.
PATIENT: I didn't mind the wait so much, but I did think you'd like to treat my illness in its early stages.

Although she had laryngitis, the woman protested loudly against the doctor's bill.
"You charged $50," she complained, "and all you did was paint my throat!"
"What did you expect?" the doctor replied. "Wallpaper?"

PATIENT: I have a splinter in my finger.
DOCTOR: That's what you get for scratching your head.

When they take out your appendix, they call it an appendectomy. When they take out your tonsils, they call it a tonsillectomy. What do they call it when they remove a growth from your head?

A haircut.

NURSE, NURSE!

PATIENT: Nurse, nurse, I keep thinking I'm a ghost!

NURSE: I thought that might be your problem when I saw you walk through the wall.

PATIENT: Nurse, nurse, I'm sick as a dog.

NURSE: I can't help you. I'm not a vet.

PATIENT: Nurse, nurse, nobody ever listens to me.

NURSE: Next!

MOTHER: Doctor, doctor, you've got to help my son! All he does is scratch himself and swing from a tree.

DOCTOR: Don't worry. He's probably just going through a phase.

MOTHER: Oh, thank you, Doctor. How much do I owe you?

DOCTOR: Thirty bananas.

SEEING SPOTS

"I've been seeing spots before my eyes lately."

"Have you seen a doctor?"

"No, just spots."

"I went to the eye doctor because I saw spots in front of my eyes. He gave me glasses."

"Did the glasses help?"

"Oh, yes. Now I can see the spots much better."

Why wouldn't the doctor allow the sick eagle in the hospital?

Because it was illegal (ill eagle)

"Have your eyes ever been checked?"
  "No, they've always been plain brown."

"Doctor, doctor, my eyesight is getting worse!"
  "You're absolutely right. This is a post office!"

DOCTOR: You need glasses.
PATIENT: But I'm already wearing glasses.
DOCTOR: In that case, I need glasses.

PATIENT: Doctor, the first 30 minutes that
  I'm up every morning, I feel dizzy.
  What should I do?
DOCTOR: Get up half an hour later.

PATIENT: Every bone in my body hurts.
DOCTOR: Be grateful you're not a sardine.

PATIENT: I think a killer bee is circling me!
DOCTOR: Oh, that's just a bug that's going
  around.

REPORTER: Doctor, what is the best thing
to do when your ear rings?
DOCTOR: Answer it.

SLEEPERS

DOCTOR: Do you always snore?
PATIENT: Only when I sleep.

Doctor: Are you a light sleeper?
Patient: No, I sleep in the dark.

Doctor: Do you sleep on your left side
or your right side?
Patient: I sleep on both sides. All of
me goes to sleep at once.

"Doctor, can I sleep in my contact
lenses?"
  "No, your feet would stick out."

REPORTER: Doctor, why do you always wear a tuxedo in the operating room?
DOCTOR: I like to dress formally for openings.

"There's a man outside in a black cape with a strange request," the nurse told the doctor.

"What does he want?" the doctor asked.

"Well, doctor," the nurse explained. "He says he wants two pints to go."

A man came into a doctor's office with two badly burned ears. "I was ironing my shirt when the phone rang," he explained. "I accidentally reached for the iron instead of the phone and put it to my ear."

"I could understand if one of your ears was burned by the iron," said the doctor, "but two?"

"Well," the man sighed, "the phone rang again."

THE BEST WAY

Patient: What's the best way to cure acid indigestion?
DOCTOR: Stop drinking acid.

PATIENT: What's the best way to avoid fallen arches?
DOCTOR: Get out of the way.

PATIENT: What's the best way to prevent wrinkles?
DOCTOR: Don't sleep in your clothes.

PATIENT: What's the best way to keep from getting fat in certain places?
DOCTOR: Stay out of those places!

DOCTOR: The best time to take this medicine is just before retiring.
PATIENT: You mean I don't have to take it until I'm 65 years old?

PATIENT: Doctor, I've got a pain in my left leg.
DOCTOR *(after examination)*: There's nothing I can do. It's old age.
PATIENT: But my left leg is just as old as my right leg and that one feels fine!

PATIENT: Will you give me something for my head?
DOCTOR: I wouldn't take it as a gift.

PATIENT: Doctor, doctor, I feel like a canary!
DOCTOR: Don't worry. Your condition is tweet-able.

DOCTOR: Strange...Your brother is very small compared to you.
PATIENT: Sure, he's my half-brother.

"Doctor, doctor, I feel warm and out of breath!"

"You must have flu."

"No, I walked over."

PATIENT: Doctor, doctor, I just swallowed a bone!

DOCTOR: Are you choking?

PATIENT: No, I'm serious!

PATIENT: I hear you are the world's greatest expert on curing baldness. If you cure me, I'll give you anything you want.

DOCTOR *(after examination)*: I have good news and bad news. The bad news is that I can't grow any more hair on your head. Now for the good news: I can shrink your head to fit the hair you've got.

113

TRACY: I have a headache. I think I'll lie down and take some aspirins.
STACY: Bayer?
TRACY: No, I'll keep my clothes on.

An angry mother took her 8-year-old to the doctor's office. "Is a boy of 8 able to perform an appendix operation?" she asked.

"Of course not," the doctor replied.

The mother turned to the little boy. "See? Now put it back!"

DOCTOR: Have you ever had that pain before?
PATIENT: Yes.
DOCTOR: Well, you've got it again.

Why did the shoe go to see the doctor?
It wanted to be healed.

PATIENT: Doctor, doctor, I work like a horse, eat like a bird, and I'm tired as a dog!
DOCTOR: Have you been to a veterinarian?

MOTHER: Doctor, doctor, you've got to help my son! He bites his nails in school.
DOCTOR: Lots of children bite their nails.
MOTHER: Their toenails?

PATIENT: You were right, Doctor, when you said you'd have me on my feet and walking around in no time.
DOCTOR: I'm happy to hear it. When did you start walking?
PATIENT: Right after I sold my car to pay your bill.

PATIENT: Doctor, doctor, I swallowed my fountain pen!
DOCTOR: What are you doing in the meantime?
PATIENT: Using a pencil.

DO THEY SUFFER?

DOCTOR: Do you suffer from rheumatism?
PATIENT: Sure, what else can you do with it?

DOCTOR: Does your family suffer from insanity?
PATIENT: No, we kind of enjoy it.

MRS. SMITH: I just came from the doctor.
MRS. JONES: Which doctor?
MRS. SMITH: No, general practitioner.

The doctors were talking about their work.

"I had great success with one of my patients," said the first doctor. "When he came to me, he thought he was as small as a mouse."

"And you cured him?"

"I convinced him that many of the world's greatest men were small," said the doctor. "He was doing quite well. Then–I lost him."

"What happened?"

"It was an accident," the doctor said sadly. "A pussy cat ate him.

PATIENT: Doctor, doctor, I've only got 59 seconds to live!

DOCTOR: Hold on, I'll be with you in a minute.

6. FUNNY FARM

Why wouldn't the chicken lay eggs?
Because he was tired of working for chickenfeed.

FARMER: Do you realize it takes 3 sheep to make one sweater?

CITY MAN: Amazing—I didn't even know they could knit.

SHAGGY CHICKEN STORY

Driving along a country road, Ronald noticed a chicken running alongside his car. He increased his speed to 45 miles an hour. The chicken kept coming. Ronald stepped on the gas, but the chicken still managed to keep up. When the car reached 55 miles an hour, the chicken passed it and turned down a dirt road. It was then that the man noticed that the chicken had 3 legs.

He followed it to a farm that was filled with 3-legged chickens.

"Say," said Ronald to the farmer, "do all your chickens have 3 legs?"

"Yep," replied the farmer. "Most people

like drumsticks, so we developed this breed."

"How do they taste?"

"Don't rightly know," answered the farmer. "Haven't been able to catch one yet."

Julie was visiting the country. Her first day on the farm, she watched the farmer's wife pluck a chicken. Finally she asked, "Do you have to take off their clothes every night?"

FARMER: Here on the farm we go to bed
   with the chickens.
CITY MAN: In the city we'd rather sleep in
   our own beds.

A family that had spent its vacation on a farm the year before wished to return. The only thing wrong with the farm was the noise made by the pigs.

The family wrote to the farmer to ask if the pigs were still there. The farmer wrote back: "Don't worry. We haven't had pigs on the farm since you were here."

A vacationer was driving along a country road when it began to rain hard. Soon the road turned to mud. Seeing a farmhouse, he knocked on the door and asked the farmer if he could stay overnight.

"Sure," said the farmer, "but you'll have to make your own bed."

"That's all right," replied the vacationer.

"Okay," said the farmer. "Here's some wood and a hammer."

SHAGGY HILLBILLY STORY

A vacationer and his family were driving through the backwoods. The man took a wrong turn and got lost. He drove miles until he came to a fork in the road. There he spotted a small shack. A hillbilly was rocking on the porch.

"Hey, there!" the vacationer called. "Can you tell me where the road on the left leads to?"

"Don't rightly know," the hillbilly replied, continuing to rock.

"Well, can you tell me where the road on the right leads to?"

"Don't know that," said the hillbilly, continuing to rock.

The vacationer got angry. "You're not very bright, are you?" he said.

"Maybe not," the hillbilly replied calmly, "but I'm not lost."

FARMER: Why are you late?
FARM HAND: I didn't look where I was going and I ran into a tree.
FARMER: That's a new one. I never heard of sap running into a tree!

"Look at that bunch of cattle."
    "Not bunch of cattle—herd."
"Heard of what?"
    "Of cattle."
"Sure, I've heard of cattle."
    "No, I mean cattle herd."
"So what? I've no secrets from them."

Did you hear about the farmer who wanted to be an astronomer? He put his cow on the scale to see how much the milky weighed (Milky Way).

BEST BULL JOKES

BESS: How can you tell if a bull is about to charge?
FESS: He takes out a credit card.

LESTER: What would you do if a bull charged you?
CHESTER: I'd pay him!

FARMER *(boasting)*: I've got thousands of cows.
VISITOR: That's a lot of cows.
FARMER: And that's not all. I've also got thousands of bulls.
VISITOR: That's a lot of bull.

VISITOR: What steps would you take if a
   bull chased you?
FARMER: Big ones!

CITY KID: Does your garden have a swing?
FARMER: No, but it has a beet.

If an apple a day keeps the doctor away,
what does an onion a day do?
It keeps everybody away.

CITY KID: How many apples grow on trees?
FARMER: All of them.

FARMER'S SON: Dad, do you like baked
apples?
FARMER: Yes, why?
FARMER'S SON: The orchard is on fire.

CITY KID: So, you run a duck farm. Is
business picking up?
FARMER: No, picking down.

CITY KID: Do you like raisin bread?
FARMER: Don't know. Never raised any.

CLEM: Did you hear the one about the
tramp who stole a rooster and a steer?
LEM: No, what about it?
CLEM: Never mind, it's a cock and bull
story.

A little girl from the city, seeing a horse being shod, rushed to her mother.

"Mother," she cried, "there's a man out there building a horse. I just saw him nailing on the feet!"

How do you make a slow horse fast?
Don't feed him.

NUT: What kind of horse has green stripes and yellow spots?

NAT: I don't know. What kind of horse?

NUT: I don't know either—that's why I asked.

The owner of a dude ranch boasted that he had the best horse in the world.

"I was riding him through the woods one day when he stumbled over a rock. I fell from the saddle and broke my leg."

"Don't tell me," the city visitor said, "that the horse reset your leg!"

"No, but he grabbed me by the belt, dragged me home, and called a doctor."

"I'm glad everything turned out so well," said the visitor.

"Not really. That dumb animal called a horse doctor."

The visitor to the dude ranch couldn't believe his eyes. A horse was playing classical music!

"How can that horse play the bass violin?" he gasped.

"No mystery," replied the dude ranch owner. "He's been taking lessons for years."

Thor, the thunder god, went to a dude ranch. After riding all day, he cried, "I'm Thor!"

His riding instructor answered, "You forgot the thaddle, thilly!"

7. THAT'S A LAUGH!

A woman went to the bank to arrange for a loan.

"I'm sorry, ma'am," the guard told her, "but the loan arranger is out to lunch."

"That's okay," said the woman. "Can I speak to Tonto?"

SAY THESE 3 TIMES QUICKLY

The bad black bug's blood.

Good blood, bad blood.

Did the thieves seize the skis?

FATHER: Marvin, why don't you play
   checkers with Franklin anymore?
MARVIN: Would you play with someone
   who lies and cheats and moves his men
   around when you're not looking?
FATHER: No, I wouldn't.
MARVIN: Well, neither would he.

MUFFY: You play checkers with your dog?
   He must be pretty smart.
DUFFY: Not really. I beat him most of the
   time.

GLENDA: I had a watch stolen from under
   my nose last night.
BRENDA: That's a funny place to wear it.

What happened after the dog swallowed a
watch?
   He got ticks.

How is Lassie like a comet?
Both are stars with tails.

"I've got a stomachache."

"That's because you haven't eaten. Your stomach is empty—that's why it hurts."

"Oh, is that why you have all those headaches?"

GLENDA: How much after midnight is it?
BRENDA: I don't know. My watch only
goes as high as 12.

Lester and Chester were riding on a train
for the first time. They had brought along
bananas to eat on the trip. Just as they
began to peel the bananas, the train
entered a dark tunnel.

"Have you eaten your banana yet?"
Lester cried.

"No," replied Chester.

"Well, don't touch it!" warned Lester. "I
took one bite and went blind!"

NIT: How do you get down from a horse?
WIT: You don't get down from a horse.
You get down from a duck.

"I gave you the best years of my life."
"So what do you want—a receipt?"

"I don't care who you are, fat man—get those reindeer off my roof!"

The goat and the farmer were shown to their seats by the theatre usher. When the film was over, the goat applauded loudly. As the goat and the farmer left the theatre, the usher asked, "And did your goat enjoy the movie?"

"Very much," the farmer said.

"Amazing!" replied the usher.

"I think so, too," said the farmer, "especially since he didn't care too much for the book."

LUCKY: I heard a new joke the other day. I wonder if I told it to you.

DUCKY: Was it funny?

LUCKY: Yes.

DUCKY: You didn't.

"I always aim to tell the truth."

"Bad shot, aren't you?"

"I found a horseshoe—that means good luck!"

"It may mean good luck to you, but some poor horse is now running around in its socks!"

A horse came into an agent's office and said, "My act is really sensational. I can fly."

The horse then flew up to the ceiling, circled the room several times, and came down in a perfect landing.

"Well? What do you think?" said the horse.

"Okay," said the agent, "you do bird imitations. But what else do you do?"

DES: I can imitate any bird you can name.
BESS: How about a homing pigeon?

TOOT: I'm worried about Herman. He's so thin.
COOT: How thin is he?
TOOT: You know how thin you are and how thin I am? Well, he's thinner than both of us put together.

WEIRDEST GHOST JOKE

Oscar got to the broken down inn and asked for a room.

"I have only one room left," said the innkeeper. "But before I give it to you, I have to tell you that room is where the white-eyed ghost lives."

Oscar wasn't worried. "I'll take the room," he said. "I'm not afraid of ghosts."

That night when Oscar went to bed, he heard a scary "Boooooo! I am the white-eyed ghost. . . ."

"Shut up," said Oscar. "I'm tired."

"Boooooooo!" the ghost said again. "I am the white-eyed ghost!"

Oscar sat up, reached over, picked up a chair and threw it at the ghost, who disappeared. Oscar lay down again and shut his eyes.

"Boooooooooo!" moaned the voice from the darkness. "I am the black-eyed ghost. . . ."

What's the difference between a coyote and a flea?

One howls on the prairie and the other prowls on the hairy.

A horse walked into a restaurant and ordered a well-done cheeseburger with onions, pickle, relish, ketchup, and mustard.

The waiter brought the food to the horse, who finished it off with great pleasure.

Noticing a cowboy staring at him as he ate, the horse said, "I suppose you think it's strange that a horse should come into a restaurant and order a well-done cheeseburger with onions, pickle, relish, ketchup, and mustard."

"Not at all," the cowboy said. "I like it that way myself."

"Did you try the meatballs?"
"Yes, I found them guilty."

GLIP: My grandfather has a wooden leg.
GLOP: That's nothing. My grandmother
has a cedar chest.

"These safety matches you sold me won't light."
"Well, you can't get much safer than that."

What's in the Great Wall of China that the Chinese didn't put in it?
Cracks.

How do tourists greet each other in Hawaii?
They say "Hawaii doing?"

"Do you always swim with your socks on?"
"Only when the water is cold."

What would you get if you crossed a comedian and a spiritualist?

A happy medium.

FLIP: Did you make that joke up out of your head?

FLOP: Absolutely.

FLIP: You must be!

DUSTY: What would you do if you found a million dollars?

RUSTY: Well, if it was a poor person who lost it, I'd return it.

RAY: Did you hear about the 12-foot-long bed?

KAY: No, what about it?

RAY: Never mind, it's a lot of bunk.

Why should you count your money on your toes?

So it doesn't slip through your fingers.

JIM: I swim with my head above water.

KIM: Sure, wood floats, doesn't it!

SAY THESE 3 TIMES QUICKLY

Brainy boys bake black bran bread.

Six sick sheiks seek sixty crisp snacks.

Should Sid shave a short single shingle thin, or shave a short thin single cedar shingle thinner?

MRS. SMITH: My, what a surprise meeting you here at the psychiatrist's office! Are you coming or going?

MRS. JONES: If I knew that I wouldn't be here.

CHARLEY: I just swallowed a frog.

FARLEY: Doesn't it make you feel sick?

CHARLEY: Sick! I'm liable to croak any minute!

BELLA: A vacuum is the dirtiest thing in nature.

DELLA: How do you know?

BELLA: Why else would they make so many cleaners for it?

LOST: Thick-lens reading glasses. Finder please advertise in LARGE PRINT.

A formation of geese was flying south for their winter vacation. One of the geese in the back complained, "How come we always have to follow that same leader?"

"Shut up!" replied another bird. "He's the one with the map."

HARRY: What was my name two days ago?
TEACHER: Harry.
HARRY: What was my name yesterday?
TEACHER: Harry.
HARRY: Knock-knock.
TEACHER: Who's there?
HARRY: See? You've forgotten me already.

TEACHER: What are you looking for in the mud?
DEXTER: I heard it rained an inch and three quarters last night. I'm looking for the quarters.

FANNY: If we breathe oxygen in the daytime, what do we breathe at night?
ANNIE: Nitrogen.

"Will you pass the nuts, teacher?"
   "No, I think I'll flunk them."

WIT: Did you hear about the man who was put in jail for stealing a pig?
NIT: How did they catch him?
WIT: The pig squealed.

ANOTHER SHAGGY HILLBILLY STORY

A motorist, travelling in the backwoods, came to a stream whose bridge had washed away. He saw a hillbilly sitting nearby whittling at a stick.

"How deep is the stream?" the motorist asked.

"Not too deep," the hillbilly said.

"Think I can drive across it?"

"Shucks, I reckon you can," said the hillbilly.

Hearing these words, the motorist drove into the stream. The car sank immediately, and the motorist barely escaped with his life.

"What do you mean by telling me I

could drive across?" the traveller said angrily. "That stream is at least 10 feet deep."

The hillbilly scratched his head. "Funny," he said, "it only reaches up to the middle of the ducks."

An undertaker was sliding a coffin into the back of a hearse when it slipped out of his hands, landed on the icy pavement, skidded down a hill, and sailed straight through the entrance to a drugstore.

As it slid past the prescription counter, the undertaker, puffing along behind, shouted to the pharmacist, "For heaven's sake, give me something to stop that coffin (coughing)!"

Harvey was on his first date with a new girl. As they drove along, she turned to him shyly and asked, "Would you like to see where I was operated on?"

Harvey gulped and said, "Why, I'd love to."

"Okay," said the girl. "We're passing the hospital now."

"May I join you?"

"Why? Am I coming apart?"

"I feel like a cup of tea."

"Strange—you don't look like one."

"I mean—may I join you in a cup of tea?"

"Absolutely not! There isn't enough room for both of us in one cup!"

"Imagine you were strapped to an operating table with Dr. Frankenstein about to transplant your brain. What would you do?"

"Quit imagining."

"Why did you wrap barbed wire around the banister in your house?"

"Junior likes to slide down banisters."

"Does the barbed wire stop him?"

"No, but it slows him down."

TEACHER: Johnny, can you tell me what they did at the Boston Tea Party?

JOHNNY: I don't know, Teacher. I wasn't invited.

CUSTOMER: There's a fly swimming in my soup. What's he doing there?

WAITER: Looks like the backstroke to me.

"Did you get the license number of the woman who ran you over?"

"No, but I'd recognize that laugh anywhere."

MOTHER: What's the idea of coming home
two hours late?

SON *(in bandages)*: But, Mom, I was run
over.

MOTHER: It doesn't take two hours to get
run over.

The sawmill boss explained to the new man how to operate the buzz saw, warning him that under no circumstances should he put his hand near the blade while the motor was running.

The first day on the job, the man put his finger in the machine and before he knew it, the finger was gone.

"What happened?" the boss said. "Didn't I show you how to operate the machine?"

"I don't understand it," the man said. "All I did was put my hand out like this—oooops! There goes another one!"

"What is the first letter in yellow?"
"Y."
"Because I want to know."

HE: Is that perfume I smell?
SHE: It is—and you do.

"Thank you so much for saving me from drowning. I'd gladly give you five dollars, but all I have is a ten dollar bill."

"That's all right. Just jump back in."

Ali Baba went up to the cave entrance and cried, "Open Sesame!"

A voice called back, "Ses who?"

"I weighed three pounds when I was born."

"You don't say! Did you live?"

"Did I! You should see me now!"

MARY: Don't you think I look like a slender birch?

GARY: No, you look more like a knotty pine.

Why did the Egyptian mummy go to the resort hotel?

It needed to unwind.

"How do you do?"

"How do I do what?"

"I mean, how do you find yourself?"

"Don't be silly. I never lose myself."

"You don't understand. How do you feel?"

"With my fingers, of course. Haven't you got anything better to do than bother me with stupid questions?"

"How can one person make so many stupid mistakes in one day?"

"I get up early."

The firing squad was escorting a prisoner to his place of execution. It was a dismal, rainy day.

"What a terrible day to die," the condemned man complained.

"What are you kicking about?" the guard said. "We have to walk all the way back in the rain!"

"If you work hard, you'll get ahead."

"No, thanks, I already have a head."

HE: I love a good old-fashioned girl.
SHE: Come over to my house and I'll
   introduce you to my grandmother.

"How did you get along with Dad while I
was away, Son?"

"Fine, Mom. Every morning he took me
down to the lake in a rowboat and let me
swim back."

"Isn't that a long way to swim?"

"The swimming wasn't too bad. The
hard part was getting out of the bag."

WOMAN *(to trash collector)*: Am I too late
   for the garbage truck?
TRASH COLLECTOR: No, lady, jump right
   in!

"When I sat down to play the piano, they all laughed."

"How come?"

"No bench."

Why was the musician arrested?
He got in treble.

WOMAN *(in art gallery)*: And this, I suppose, is one of those hideous monstrosities you call modern art?

ART DEALER: No, madam, it's a mirror.

JANE: I've seen your face somewhere before.

SHANE: How odd.

JANE: Yes, it certainly is.

"Are you the wonderfully brave young man who tried to save my son's life when he broke through the ice on the lake?"

"Yes, ma'am."

"Well, where did you hide his mittens?"

"Does anyone on board know how to pray?"

"I do."

"Good—you pray. The rest of us will put on life vests. We're one short."

The man received a sinister note saying, "Give us $50,000 or you will never see your wife again."

"I don't have the money," the man replied, "but your proposition interests me."

"You and your suicide attempts! Just look at this gas bill!"

Read in the will of a miserly millionaire:
"...And to my dear nephew Sam, whom I promised to remember in my will, 'Hi, there, Sam!'"

The businessman lay on his deathbed.

"I have a confession to make," he sobbed to his partner. "I robbed our firm of $100,000. I sold our business secrets to our competitors. I stole merchandise. I lied and cheated and –"

"That's all right, old man," said his partner. "It was me who poisoned you."

8. CAMPING OUT

"Lucilla, what's the definition of 'intense'?"
"That's where campers sleep."

NICK: If you were hunting in the woods and met a bear, would you give him both barrels?
VIC: I'd give him the whole gun!

BROWNIE LEADER: Why do bears live in caves?
BROWNIE: They can't afford apartments in the city.

OUTDOOR BOOKSHELF

Mountain Climbing
by Cliff Hanger

Growing Spices
by Herb Gardner

Living in the Woods
by Sir Vyval

Cookouts Italian Style
by Liz Anya, Manny Cotie, Minna
Stroney, and Lynne Gweeny

GLORIA: What would you get if you crossed a vampire and a camp counselor?

GLENN: I don't know, but I wouldn't want to be in his cabin.

HE: You bring out the beast in me.
SHE: I know—a jackass.

BUCK: If you were hiking in the woods and saw a bear heading for you, would you keep walking—or would you run back to town?

CHUCK: I'd run back to town.

BUCK: With a bear behind?

EAGLE SCOUT: What would you do if a bear came after you while you were hiking through the woods?

TENDERFOOT: I'd climb a tree.

EAGLE SCOUT: That's not smart. Bears can climb trees.

TENDERFOOT: Not this tree. It would be shaking too hard.

Did you hear about the camper who backed into the campfire? He burned his britches behind him.

"Mommy, what's a werewolf?"
    "Shut up, Kid, and comb your face."

One Sunday a camper went swimming in the river. When he wanted to come back on shore, he couldn't. Why not?

The banks are closed on Sunday.

Why can't it rain for two nights in a row?

Because there is a day in between.

What did the dust say to the rain?

"If this keeps up, my name will be Mud."

Two hikers were sitting around a campfire when a huge grizzly bear suddenly appeared in front of them.

"Keep calm," said the first hiker. "Remember what we read in that book. If you stay absolutely still and look the bear straight in the eye, he won't attack you."

"I don't know about that," said the other hiker. "You've read the book and I've read the book—but has the bear read the book?"

Why do squirrels spend so much time in the trees?

To keep away from the nuts on the ground.

COUNSELOR: Trudy, what are you going to do in the camp talent show?

TRUDY: Imitations.

COUNSELOR: Great–let's hear one.

TRUDY: I love you–ouch! I love you–ouch!

COUNSELOR: I give up. Who are you imitating?

TRUDY: Two porcupines kissing.

FATHER: What did you get that little medal for?

RINGO: For singing in the camp talent show.

FATHER: What did you get that big medal for?

RINGO: For stopping.

FIRST CAMPER: It sure is dark tonight.

SECOND CAMPER: I'll say. I just saw an owl wearing eyeglasses.

CAMP COUNSELOR: Can owls see on very dark nights?

CAMPER: Yes, but they have a lot of trouble holding the flashlight.

MOTHER: I don't want those flies around the picnic table. Please shoo them, Hector.

HECTOR: Oh, Mom, let them go barefoot.

TRIXIE: How many of your relatives came to the picnic?

DIXIE: Three uncles and about 100,000 aunts.

YOU: When I was in camp this summer, I stood underwater for ten minutes.
(When the person you tell this to says it's impossible, show him how. Put a glass of water over your head and stand under it.)

CUSTOMER: Give me some cockroach powder, please.
CLERK: Shall I wrap it up?
CUSTOMER: No, I'll send the roaches down to eat it here.

NEW CAMPER: Is the food in this camp any good?

CAMPER: Sure, if you happen to be a termite.

FATHER: How did you like camp as a whole, Terry?

TERRY: As a hole it was all right, but as a camp it was terrible.

Did you hear about the silly camper who bought a sleeping bag? He spent three weeks trying to wake it up.

FATHER: Now, Michael, be good while you're away at camp.

MICHAEL: Okay, Dad, I'll be good for ten dollars.

FATHER: Why, son, when I was your age, I was good for nothing.

CAMP COUNSELOR: What are you taking
  home from camp—the train or the bus?
CAMPER: I don't think either one would fit
  through the door.

MOTHER *(helping to unpack camp trunk)*:
Freddie, I'm so proud of you! You got
awards for hiking, sailing, nature, and
arts and crafts. But tell me, what is this
medal for?

FREDDIE: It's for having my trunk packed
neatly when we came home.

MOTHER: That's wonderful! How did you
do it?

FREDDIE: I never unpacked.

CAMP COUNSELOR: Why are you putting
two quarters under your pillow?

CAMPER: Those are my sleeping quarters.

CAMP COUNSELOR: Seymour—get up! It's
seven o'clock! The birds have been
awake for hours.

SEYMOUR *(still sleepy)*: If I had to sleep on
a tree branch, I'd get up early, too.

What kind of camper would you get if you crossed a porcupine and a young goat?

A stuck-up kid.

SANDY: What do you get if you cross a gopher and a porcupine?
MANDY: I have no idea.
SANDY: A tunnel that leaks.

Larry and Harry went on an overnight hike. They came to a river.

"How are we going to get across?" Larry asked. "We don't have a boat."

"I know," said Harry. "I'll shine my flashlight over the river and you can cross on the beam."

"Oh, no," said Larry. "I'd only get halfway and you'd turn the flashlight off!"

"How do you know you're eating rabbit stew?"

"It has hares in it."

BOY: Doc, my pet rabbit is sick. I can't understand it. I rub him down with vaseline every day.

VET: No wonder! Don't you know you're not supposed to use that greasy stuff on your hare?

What do you have if a bird and a dog get into the camp loudspeaker system?
A tweeter and a woofer.

CAMPER: I have the feeling that no one in camp gives a hoot for me.
COUNSELOR: So?

CAMPER: No one likes me.
COUNSELOR: Why do you say that, you boring little creep?

SARAH: Timmy's parents sent him to camp.
LOUELLA: Did he need a vacation?
SARAH: No, they did.

9. GOING PLACES

JECKLE: I'm going on a safari to Africa.
HECKLE: Drop us a lion.

HECKLE: How is the safari going?
JECKLE: Safari so good.

Did you hear about the frog who parked
his car illegally?
   It got toad away.

On their way to the seashore, a trainer and his talking dog were speeding along in a new sports car. A police car started after them.

"Pull over to the side," said the dog. "And when he gets here, let me do all the talking."

Speeding Motorist: Was I driving too fast?

State Trooper: No, you were flying too low.

While driving cross-country, a driver noticed a large sign above a gas station. It read, "State line 2 miles. Last chance for 92 cent gas."

The driver checked his gas gauge and decided to fill up.

"By the way," he said to the attendant before driving away, "just how much is gas in the next state?"

"Oh," said the attendant, "about 80 cents a gallon."

A man driving an old wreck of a car drove up to a toll booth.

"One dollar," said the toll collector.

"Sold!" said the driver.

Lem and Clem had locked the key inside their car.

"Why don't we get a coat hanger to open it?" Lem asked.

"No," answered Clem. "People will think we're trying to break in."

A few minutes later, Lem said, "What if we use my pocketknife to cut around the rubber and then stick a finger in and pull up the lock?"

"No, no," said Clem. "People will think we're too dumb to use a coat hanger."

"Well," sighed Lem, "we'd better think of something fast. It's starting to rain and the sunroof is open!"

A motorist was driving a big black car down a country lane. His lights were not on. The moon was not out. A sheep was crossing the road. How did the driver see the sheep?

It was a bright sunny day.

FLIP: Do Cadillacs stretch?
FLOP: No, but Mercedes Benz.

What would you get if you crossed an airplane, an automobile, and a dog?

A flying car-pet.

What would you get if you crossed a 747 and a magician?

A flying sorcerer.

WORLD'S
SILLIEST
MOUNTAIN-CLIMBING JOKE

The two mountain climbers had reached the end of their exhausting journey. Though at the point of collapse, they made it to the top.

"It almost cost us our lives to climb this mountain," the first climber said, "but it will be worth it to plant our country's flag on the top. This is the proudest moment of my life. Please—hand me the flag."

The second mountain climber stared at him in surprise and said, "I thought you brought it!"

FATHER: Now, Michael, don't be selfish. Let your sister have the sled half the time.

MICHAEL: I do, Dad. I have it going downhill and she has it going up.

BETH: I fell down a dozen times while I was skating today. I was so embarrassed.

SETH: Why? Did anyone laugh at you?

BETH: Well, the ice cracked up!

SUE: It's going to be tough sledding today.

DREW: Why is that?

SUE: No snow.

CLERK *(at ski lodge to registering guest)*: Just your name, address, and Blue Cross number, please.

Jed and Ted decided to explore the countryside on a two-seater bike. They came to a hill. The going was hard. At last they got to the top.

With short breath and a perspiring face, Jed said, "That was a tough hill, but we finally made it!"

"Yes," said Ted. "Luckily, I had my hand on the brake. Otherwise, we would have rolled all the way down!"

TOMMY: I played soccer yesterday and sprained my leg. That's why I was absent from school.
TEACHER: Of all the lame excuses!

NIT: I played hockey last week and broke an arm and a leg.
WIT: Some people get all the breaks!

GOOD NEWS/
BAD NEWS JOKE

At a championship high diving contest, a spectacular dive was performed to wild applause. Then the announcer's voice came over the loudspeaker:

"Ladies and gentlemen! I have some good news and some bad news. The good news is that the judges have awarded the magnificent dive you just witnessed a perfect score. The bad news is— there was no water in the pool."

What's the difference between a bird and a fly?

A bird can fly, but a fly can't bird.

Why do birds fly south?

Because if they walked, it would be winter by the time they got there.

Did you hear the joke about the airplane?
Never mind, it just took off.

REPORTER: What made you take up the sport of sky diving?

PARACHUTIST: A four-engine aircraft with three dead engines.

"And then, thousands of feet above the ground, I pulled the string. I knew that should my parachute fail to open, I would dash my poor brains out on the ground below."

"And–did you?"

A pesty child was making a nuisance of himself by playing ball in a plane that was crossing the ocean.

"Listen, kid," said one of the passengers, "why don't you go outside and play?"

What kind of flying school doesn't anyone want to go to?

One that has a crash course.

It was the boy's first trip by plane. As the engines began to roar, he gripped the arms of his seat, closed his eyes, and counted to 100.

When he opened his eyes, he looked out the window.

"See those tiny people down there?" he said to the woman sitting next to him. "Don't they look like ants?"

"They are ants," the woman said. "We haven't left the ground yet."

10. IT'S ALL IN YOUR HEAD

FARMER: Doctor, doctor, my wife thinks she's a chicken!

DOCTOR: How long has this been going on?

FARMER: Three years.

DOCTOR: Why didn't you bring her to me sooner?

FARMER: We needed the eggs.

PATIENT: Can a person be in love with an elephant?

DOCTOR: Impossible!

PATIENT: Do you know anyone who wants to buy a very large engagement ring?

PATIENT: Doctor, I haven't been able to sleep for a week. Every night I dream of a door with a sign on it. I push and push—but I still can't open that door.

DOCTOR: What does the sign say?

PATIENT: "Pull."

PSYCHIATRIST: What did you dream about last night?

PATIENT: Baseball.

PSYCHIATRIST: Baseball—always baseball! Don't you ever dream about anything else?

PATIENT: What? And miss my turn at bat?

DOCTOR: What is your problem?

PATIENT: I like bow ties.

DOCTOR: Is that all? Thousands of people like bow ties. I prefer them myself.

PATIENT: You do? What a relief! How do you like them—boiled or fried?

WIFE: Doctor, doctor, my husband thinks he's a chocolate bar!

DOCTOR: Good. That means he's only half nuts.

DOCTOR, DOCTOR!

WIFE: Doctor, doctor, my husband
thinks he's a refrigerator!
DOCTOR: If that's his only problem,
don't worry about it.
WIFE: But he sleeps with his mouth
open and the light keeps me up all
night.

WIFE: Doctor, doctor, my husband
thinks he's an elevator!
DOCTOR: I'll see him. Send him up.
WIFE: I can't. He doesn't stop at your
floor.

PATIENT: Doctor, doctor, I think I'm a dog!

DOCTOR: Sit!

PATIENT: Doctor, doctor, I think I'm a dog!

DOCTOR: How long has this been going on?

PATIENT: Ever since I was a puppy.

PATIENT: Doctor, doctor, I think I'm a dog!

PSYCHIATRIST: Please lie down on the couch.

PATIENT: I can't. I'm not allowed on the furniture.

"For months I thought I was a dog, but my psychiatrist cured me."

"How are you now?"

"Fine. Feel my nose."

PATIENT: Doctor, doctor, I feel like an
elephant!
DOCTOR: Tusk, tusk.

WIFE: Doctor, doctor, my husband thinks he's a washing machine!

DOCTOR: What's so bad about that?

WIFE: He isn't getting the clothes clean.

HUSBAND: Doctor, doctor, my wife thinks she's a parking meter!

DOCTOR: My goodness, let me see her right away.

HUSBAND: She can't come in until next Tuesday. That's when the meter maid takes the money out of her mouth.

PATIENT: Doctor, doctor, I feel like a duck!

DOCTOR: I can give you an appointment next month.

PATIENT: I can't wait. I have to fly south for the winter.

PATIENT: Doctor, doctor, I keep thinking
    I'm a bridge!
DOCTOR: What's come over you?
PATIENT: So far, four cars and two trucks.

DOCTOR: Mr. Johnson, I think you're
  suffering from a split personality.
MR. JOHNSON: No, we're not.

PATIENT: Doctor, doctor, I've got a complex!
DOCTOR: I was a-Freud of that.

DOCTOR: About this habit of talking to
  yourself—it's nothing to worry about.
PATIENT: Well, maybe not, but I'm such an
  awful bore.

PATIENT: Doctor, doctor, I have the feeling
  that people don't care what I say.
DOCTOR: So?

PATIENT: D-d-d-oc-oc-oc-t-t-or, d-d-d-oc-
  oc-t-t-or, I—I—ha-ha-ha-ve trou-bbb-bbb-
  ll ss-ss-sp-eak-eak-in-g.
DOCTOR: Sorry, I wasn't listening. What
  was that again?

PATIENT: Doctor, doctor, I keep thinking there are two of me!

DOCTOR: Say that again, and this time don't both speak at once.

PATIENT: Doctor, doctor, I feel better today! The only thing still bothering me is my breathing!

DOCTOR: Don't worry, we'll put a stop to that!

PSYCHIATRIST *(to nurse)*: Please just say we are very busy—not that it's a madhouse!

HUSBAND: Doctor, doctor, every day my wife tries to wash the car!

DOCTOR: What's wrong with that? Most husbands would love to have their wives wash the car.

HUSBAND: In the bathtub?

PSYCHIATRIST *(correcting patient)*:
No one who can afford my fees can be a total failure.

A patient was complaining to a friend: "After two years and $10,000, my psychiatrist told me I was cured. Some cure! Two years ago I was George Washington—and now who am I? A nobody!"

PATIENT: Thanks for curing me of gambling, doc. You did a great job.
PSYCHIATRIST: Thank you. Here's my bill.
PATIENT: I'll toss you for it—double or nothing!

11. ALL WET!

Four-year-old Jeannie, visiting her aunt's summer cottage, was watching a couple of waterskiers on the lake. Turning to her aunt, she said, "Those guys are so dumb! They're never going to catch up with that boat!"

SWIMMING INSTRUCTOR: Swimming is one
of the best exercises for keeping slim.
LIZZIE: Did you ever see a whale?

"How do I start the motor of this boat?"

"All it takes is a jerk on the cord. You're
perfect for the job."

What kind of pool can't you swim in?
A car pool.

A call came into the Coast Guard station in a resort area. "Save us, save us!" cried a voice. "We're inexperienced sailors and we're ten miles from shore!"

The radio operator quickly asked, "Capsize?"

A delay followed. "Uh, 6 and 7/8," came the reply.

CAPTAIN: This boat makes 20 knots an hour.
PASSENGER: Wow! How long does it take to untie them?

BLABBERMOUTH: I never learned to swim.
SWIMMING COACH: Of course. You couldn't keep your mouth closed long enough!

GOOD NEWS/BAD NEWS

SLAVEMASTER *(to Roman galley slaves who have been pulling on the oars for hours)*: I have some good news and some bad news. The good news is that you can have a 15-minute rest. The bad news is that at the end of the rest period, the captain wants to go waterskiing.

CY: I've been swimming since I was five.
HY: Gosh, you must be tired!

Stanley: Did you know I was a life saver at the beach last year?
SHIRLEY: Really? What flavor?

Will: I'm going canoeing.
JILL: Why are you carrying a gun?
WILL: I'm going to shoot the rapids.

Chip: Did you hear the joke about the swan dive?
CHOP: No.
CHIP: That's swan on you!

Seth: Would you like to see me take a dive off that high diving board?
BETH: Sure.
SETH: And I thought you were a friend of mine!

Homer agreed to take care of his little sister Suzy while his parents went shopping. He asked if he could take her fishing, and they said it was all right.

"I'll never take her fishing with me again," Homer complained to his parents when they got home. "I didn't catch a single fish."

"I'm sure she'll be quiet next time," his mother said. "Just explain that the fish swim away when there's noise."

"It wasn't the noise," Homer said. "She ate the bait!"

Clem and Lem were fishing. For three hours neither of them moved a muscle. Then Lem shifted his foot a couple of times. Clem grumbled, "That's the second time you've moved your foot in 20 minutes. Did you come here to fish or to dance?"

TIP: I was down at the lake and I saw a catfish.

TOP: Really? How did it hold the rod?

You know what fishing is?
It's when a jerk on one
end of the line waits for
a jerk on the other.

GAME WARDEN: Can't you read that sign?
It says "No Fishing Allowed"!

FISHERMAN: Oh, but I'm fishing silently.

Old fishermen never die—they just smell
that way.

FIRST FISHERMAN: Is this a good lake for fish?

SECOND FISHERMAN: It must be terrific. I can't get any of them to come out.

NICK: How's the fishing around here?

RICK: Fine.

NICK: Then how come you haven't caught anything?

RICK: You asked me about the fishing, not the catching.

GAME WARDEN: Don't you know you can't fish without a permit?

BOY: That's all right, mister. I'm doing fine with these worms.

GAME WARDEN: You fishing?

FISHERMAN: No, just drowning worms.

SHOPPER: I'm going on a fishing trip and I'd like to buy some tackle. Please hurry–I have to catch a bus!

CLERK: I'm sorry, sir, we don't have fishing tackle that big.

Marvin had been fishing all day without any luck. On the way home he stopped at a fish market and said to the clerk, "Please stand there and throw me a few of your biggest trout."

The clerk was puzzled. "Throw them to you? What for?"

"I may be a poor fisherman," Marvin replied, "but I'm no liar. I want to be able to say I caught them myself."

A fisherman tried several different kinds of bait without getting a single bite. Finally, in disgust, he threw a handful of coins into the lake.

"Okay, wise guys!" he shouted to the fish. "Go out and buy something you like!"

12. LAW & ORDER

SHERIFF: Can you hit that circle with your rifle?

DEPUTY: No, sir, I'm a square shooter.

SHERIFF: How many shots did the outlaw fire at you?

DEPUTY: Two shots. One when the bullet passed me and one when I passed the bullet.

Why did the sharpshooter carry a ruler?
So he could shoot straight.

SHERIFF: If you had
a gun with only
one bullet and an
outlaw was coming
at you from the
north and another from
the south, which would
you shoot?

DEPUTY: I'd shoot the gun.

SAY THESE 3 TIMES QUICKLY

Good gunsmoke–bad gunsmoke.

Sharpshooters should shoot slowly.

Should sheriffs sup at cheap chop suey shops?

PRISONER # 1: I'm in jail because I made big money.

PRISONER # 2: How much?

PRISONER # 1: About a quarter of an inch too big.

DEPUTY: Are you going to the big hanging today?

TOURIST: Oh, no! Where do they do things like that?

DEPUTY: At the art gallery. They're going to hang a bunch of pictures.

A Cub Scout troop visited the Sheriff's office and saw pictures of "Wanted" outlaws on the wall. One little boy pointed to a picture and asked if that really was the photograph of the wanted outlaw. The Sheriff said it was.

"Then why," asked the little boy, "didn't you keep him when you took his picture?"

SHERIFF: How could you let the outlaw escape?

DEPUTY: I couldn't help it, Sheriff. He stepped on a scale and got a weigh.

SHERIFF: The outlaw got away, eh? Didn't you guard the exits like I told you?

DEPUTY: Yes, I did, Sheriff. But the outlaw tricked me. He went out through the entrance.

SHERIFF: How could you let the outlaw get away from you in broad daylight?

DEPUTY: I couldn't help it, Sheriff. He ran into a movie theatre.

SHERIFF: Why didn't you run in after him?

DEPUTY: I would have, but I already saw the movie.

That outlaw's so tough, when he wants tea, he swallows a mouthful of water and a tea bag and sits on a hot stove until the water boils.

DEPUTY: What's the new prisoner like?
SHERIFF: He's mean, low, nasty, dirty, rotten... and those are just his good points.

SHERIFF: Deputy, deputy! Where are you?
DEPUTY: I'm here, hiding in the closet.
SHERIFF: What are you doing there?
DEPUTY: You told me to read Dr. Jekyll
  and Hyde.

What would you get if you crossed Jesse James and Count Dracula?

A robbery at the blood bank.

BIFF: What is the difference between a six-shooter and a toothpick?

CLIFF: What?

BIFF: Well, if you don't know, better not pick your teeth.

FIRST LITTLE BOY: My uncle can shoot a gun faster than any man in the West. He can even shoot without taking his gun out of its holster.

SECOND LITTLE BOY: What do you call your uncle?

FIRST LITTLE BOY: "Toeless Joe."

DEPUTY: That's a strange-looking dog.

SHERIFF: He's a genuine police dog.

DEPUTY: He doesn't look like any police dog I've ever seen.

SHERIFF: Of course not. He's in the secret service.

What about the dog that got thrown out of the flea circus?

He stole the show.

SHERIFF *(standing over the body of an outlaw named Juan)*: He must have been shot with a golf gun.

DEPUTY: What's a golf gun?

SHERIFF: The gun that made a hole in Juan (hole in one).

BESTSELLERS IN DODGE CITY

Dirty Crooks
by Phil T. Hans & Nita Bath

Crime Doesn't Pay
by Landon Jale

Catching Rustlers
by Calder Pallese

How to Become a Successful Outlaw
by Robin Steele

FLAP: My brother was doing all right until they caught up with him.

JACK: I didn't know your brother was a crook.

FLAP: He isn't. He's a race car driver.

JUDGE: Have you ever held up a train?

OUTLAW: Now and then.

JUDGE: Where did you hold up trains?

OUTLAW: Here and there.

JUDGE: What things have you taken from passengers?

OUTLAW: This and that.

JUDGE: Sheriff, lock this man up!

OUTLAW: Hey! When do I get out of jail?

JUDGE: Oh, sooner or later.

JUDGE: You look familiar. Have you ever been up before me?

CRIMINAL: I don't know. What time do you get up?

What would you get if two outlaw gangs
entered a sky diving contest?

A chute out.

JUDGE: I must charge you with murder.
DEFENDANT: Okay, what do I owe you?

BOB: I got fired from my job as bank guard today.

SLOB: How come?

BOB: A masked bandit came into the bank. I drew my gun and told him that if he took one more step, I'd let him have it.

SLOB: What did he do?

BOB: He took one more step, so I let him have it. Who wanted that dumb old gun, anyway?

13. JOCK & JILL

DIS: Your mother and father must have lifted weights.

DAT: What makes you say that?

DIS: How else could they have raised a big dumbbell like you?

What does the Invisible Man call his mother and father?

His transparents.

I didn't say you were a crack tennis player.
I just said you were cracked.

Your feet are so big, you don't need skis to
go waterskiing.

Overheard on the golf course:
GOLFER: You've got to be the world's
  worst caddy.
CADDY: Well, how's that for a coincidence!

BIFF: I have the body of an athlete.
CLIFF: Better give it back. You're getting it
  out of shape.

PAT: I'm on my way to try out for the
  school swimming team.
RAT: Are you joking? You can barely fight
  the current when you let out the bath
  water.

Why don't you stop by the pool? I'd like to give you drowning lessons.

CANDY: The national sport in Spain is
  bullfighting, and in England it's cricket.
MANDY: I'd rather play in England.
CANDY: Why?
MANDY: I'd rather fight crickets.

NIP: You'd make a great football player.
TUCK: Really?
NIP: Yes, even your breath is offensive.

Did you hear about the athlete who tried out for the track team? He couldn't even jump to a conclusion.

Did you hear about the athlete who tried out for the pole vault? He could barely clear his throat.

That uniform fits you like a glove—a boxing glove.

You're in shape, all right—the wrong shape!

If your body were a building, it would be condemned.

HOW WEAK AM I?

You're so weak, you couldn't even bend a wet noodle.

You're so weak, you couldn't even beat a rug.

You're so weak, if you played a piano, the piano would win.

You're so weak, if you beat an egg, we'd all be surprised.

You remind me of a relief pitcher. If I don't have to look at you, it's a relief.

You remind me of a racquetball game. You're off the wall.

You remind me of a shortstop. You've been off base all your life.

You remind me of a basketball player. You dribble all over yourself.

YOU'RE IN SUCH BAD SHAPE—

HOW BAD IS IT?

You're in such bad shape, you breathe hard when your stocking runs.

You're in such bad shape, you couldn't even strike a match.

You're in such bad shape, I hear undertakers come up to you and give estimates.

YOU'RE IN SUCH BAD SHAPE—

HOW BAD IS IT?

You're in such bad shape, if a vampire bit you, all it would get is practice.

You're in such bad shape, if you tried to run a bath, you'd come in second.

You're in such bad shape, you look like you're walking around just to save on funeral expenses.

YOU'RE SO LAZY—

HOW LAZY AM I?

You're so lazy, the only exercise you get is running people down.

You're so lazy, the only time you move fast is when you run a fever.

You're so lazy, you wait for the wind to blow your nose.

You're so lazy, the only thing you do fast is get tired.

YIP: I was great in sports when I was
young. I had the body of an athlete.
YAP: Well, you still have the feet.

According to a new scientific theory,
lifting weights kills germs. The only
problem is getting the germs to lift
weights.

VICKIE: My father can hold up ten cars
and a truck.
NICKIE: He must be the world's greatest
weightlifter.
VICKIE: No, he's a traffic cop.

FLIM: My brother works out with weights.
He's so strong, this morning he tore a
telephone book in half.
FLAM: That's nothing. My brother's so
strong, this morning he rushed out the
door and tore up the street.

Your shape isn't half bad—it's all bad.

GIG: I can bend bars with my bare hands.
WIG: Sure, chocolate bars.

Some people can tear a telephone book
apart. You'd have trouble with a wet
Kleenex.

MUTT: I'm going to the blood bank.
JEFF: Don't bother. They want blood, not
    crud.

14. HOSPITAL HI-JINX

DOCTOR: I'd like to take your appendix
out tomorrow.
PATIENT: Well, okay, but make sure you
get it home by eleven.

PATIENT: Doctor, doctor, a crate of eggs
fell on my head!
DOCTOR: Well, the yolk's on you!

NURSE: Doctor, you've got to learn not to cut so deeply. That's the third table you've ruined this month!

DOCTOR: Shall I give you a local anesthetic?
PATIENT: No, I'd prefer something imported.

FLIP: How did it feel when they sewed you up after the operation?
FLOP: Oh, sew-sew.

"I had an operation and the doctor left a sponge in me."
   "Got any pain?"
"No, but, boy, do I get thirsty!"

What was the surgeon doing in church?
   An organ transplant.

259

PATIENT: I'm nervous, Doctor. This is my first operation.

DOCTOR: I know how you feel. This is my first one, too.

PATIENT: How much will the operation cost?

DOCTOR: A thousand dollars.

PATIENT: A thousand dollars! Can't you do it for less?

DOCTOR: Sorry, that's a cut rate price.

Old surgeons don't die—they just cut out.

PATIENT: You've helped me a lot, doctor. A year ago, when the phone rang, I wouldn't have answered it.

DOCTOR: You've made great progress.

PATIENT: That's right. Today I answer the phone whether it rings or not.

Don't think of it as being in the hospital for an operation. Think of it as being recalled by the factory.

PATIENT: Nurse, please bring me a hot water bottle. My toes are as cold as ice.

NURSE *(insulted)*: You're asking the wrong nurse. I happen to be the head nurse.

PATIENT: Okay, would you send in the foot nurse?

PATIENT: Nurse, my feet are frozen and they're sticking out from under the covers.

NURSE: Why don't you pull them in?

PATIENT: No way! I'm not putting those cold things in bed with me!

KURT: He's an M.D.
BURT: Medical doctor?
KURT: No, Mental Defective.

MAY I HAVE A GLASS OF WATER?

PATIENT: May I have a glass of water?
NURSE: To drink?
PATIENT: No, I want to rinse out a few things.

PATIENT: May I have a glass of water?
NURSE: To drink?
PATIENT: No, I want to practice my high diving act.

PATIENT: May I have a glass of water?
NURSE: Are you thirsty?
PATIENT: No, I want to see if my neck leaks.

JUNIOR: Dad, may I have another glass of
    water before I go to sleep?
DAD: What, another? This is your tenth!
JUNIOR: I know, but my room is on fire.

PATIENT: May I have a glass of water?
NURSE: To drink?
PATIENT: No, I want to go water skiing.

BILLY: My father has been in the hospital
    for years.
GILLY: What's the matter with him?
BILLY: Nothing. He's a doctor.

Sitting in his hospital bed, a hunter was
bragging about how he single-handedly
took on a bear he met in the woods.
    "So then, when I finally got my wrist
firmly wedged between his teeth, I threw
him down on top of me and started
beating him senseless with my face."

DOCTOR: Where do you bathe?
FARMER: In the spring.
DOCTOR: I didn't ask you when, I asked
    you where.

A man was bitten by his pet cobra and taken to the hospital.

The doctor asked, "Did you see the cobra before it bit you?"

"Yes," sighed the man. "I knew him poisonally."

A waiter suddenly became ill and was rushed to the hospital. He was lying on the operating table in extreme pain when he saw an intern go by.

"Doctor, help me!" pleaded the waiter.

"Sorry," replied the intern. "That isn't my table."

PATIENT: If I stand on my head, all my blood rushes into it. Why doesn't all my blood rush into my feet when I stand on them?

DOCTOR: Your feet aren't empty.

PATIENT: Doctor, doctor, I can't sleep at night. I've tried all kinds of remedies, but nothing works.

DOCTOR: Have you tried talking to yourself?

Have you ever thought of having yourself X-rayed? I'd like to find out what you see in you.

"How is your health these days?"

"I sleep soundly and eat like a horse."

"Let's leave your table manners out of this."

Did you hear the joke about the food in this hospital? Never mind—it would only turn your stomach.

The food in this hospital is so bad, flies only eat it when they want to commit suicide.

NEW PATIENT: Is the food in this hospital any good?

OLD PATIENT: Sure, if you happen to be a termite.

VISITOR: How is the hospital food?

PATIENT: I'd rather not say—but you get a prescription with every meal.

NURSE: We have two dinners today. Take your pick.

PATIENT: No, thanks, I'll take my hammer.

FIRST COCKROACH: That hospital is the cleanest place I ever saw. The floors are gleaming, the ceilings are spotless, and everything is germ-free.

SECOND COCKROACH: Please—not while I'm eating!

ARE YOU AWAKE?

NURSE: Are you awake?
PATIENT: No, I'm having 20 winks.
NURSE: You mean 40 winks, don't you?
PATIENT: No, I'm only half asleep.

NURSE: Wake up! Wake up!
PATIENT *(startled from sleep)*: Huh?
  What's the matter?
NURSE: I forgot to give you your
  sleeping pills!

PATIENT: I woke up this morning with
  my head spinning and everything
  going round and round.
NURSE: Oh, you slept like a top!

271

PATIENT: I didn't sleep a wink.
NURSE: Did you try counting sheep?
PATIENT: I couldn't see them—it was too
  dark.

PATIENT: Doctor, doctor, can I get rid of
fat where I have it most?
DOCTOR: Sure, but you'd look ridiculous
walking around without your head.

PATIENT: Doctor, doctor, I'm getting more
and more forgetful lately.
DOCTOR: When did you first notice this
problem?
PATIENT: What problem?

Little Freddie became ill and was taken to
the hospital. It was his first time away
from home and he began to cry.

"What's the matter, Freddie?" asked the
nurse. "Are you homesick?"

"No," sobbed Freddie. "I'm *here* sick."

You remind me of medicine—thick, bitter,
and hard to take.

PATIENT: Doctor, tell me, what does the X-ray of my head show?

DOCTOR: Nothing, I'm afraid.

PATIENT: Doctor, doctor, that ointment you gave me makes my arm smart!

DOCTOR: Why don't you try putting some on your head?

MEDICAL PUTDOWNS

If you had a brain transplant, the brain would reject you.

In your case, a brain operation would be minor surgery.

I hear you went to see a lot of doctors about your brain, but they couldn't find anything.

Sick? If they gave you a blood test, you'd fail.

You look like you went to the blood bank and forgot to say "when."

You're so sick, anyone who goes with you needs a prescription.

PATIENT: Doctor, doctor, something is preying on my mind!
DOCTOR: Don't worry. It's sure to starve to death.

15. BITE DOWN HARD

PATIENT: What do you charge for pulling a tooth?

DENTIST: Fifty dollars.

PATIENT: Fifty dollars for a couple of minutes work?

DENTIST: Well, I could do it slower.

DENTIST: I was just admiring that cavity in your lower molar.

STUART: Is it that bad?

DENTIST: I've seen bears come out of smaller holes.

BOOKS FOR DENTISTS

Fighting Cavities
by Moe Lehr and Phil M. Upp

Dentistry Self-Taught
by Yank M. Goode

Dental Examinations
by Hope N. Wide

Happy Teeth
by Payne Les Dennis Tree

"Good grief!" said the dentist. "You've got the biggest cavity I've ever seen–the biggest cavity I've ever seen!"

"You don't have to repeat yourself," snapped the patient.

"I didn't," said the dentist. "That was the echo."

The dentist was about to leave his office, golf bag on his shoulder, when the phone rang.

"Doctor," said the caller, "I have a terrible toothache. Can I stop by your office for a few minutes?"

"Sorry," replied the dentist, "I'm booked up. I have to fill up 18 cavities this afternoon."

What's a dentist's favorite game?
Tooth or consequences.

DENTIST *(on the golf course, about to putt the ball into the hole)*: Open wide!

When the dentist walked up to his patient, the patient let out a yell.

"What are you hollering for?" the dentist asked. "You're not even in the chair yet."

"I know, Doc," the patient answered, "but you're standing on my toe."

DENTIST: What kind of filling would you like?
JULIE: Do you have strawberry?

"I told you not to swallow!" yelled the dentist. "That was my last pair of pliers!"

HENRIETTA: Doctor, I chipped my tooth eating animal crackers.
DENTIST: But animal crackers are soft.
HENRIETTA: Not these—they were dog biscuits.

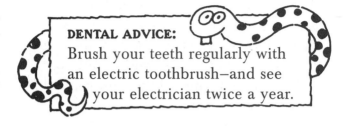

DENTAL ADVICE:
Brush your teeth regularly with an electric toothbrush—and see your electrician twice a year.

Why didn't the man buy an electric toothbrush?
Because he didn't have any electric teeth.

COWARD: I've come in to see the dentist.
NURSE: I'm sorry, but he's out right now.
COWARD: Good! When do you expect him to be out again?

DENTIST: I see you've lost your two front teeth.
ALBERT: No, I haven't. I have them in my pocket.

MOREY: I like to go to the dentist.

LORI: You really *like* to see the dentist?

MOREY: Yes. My teacher, my mother, my big sister—they all tell me to shut up. The dentist is the only person who tells me to open my mouth!

PATIENT *(at dentist's door)*: Hello, Doc. Glad to see you. *(He goes.)*

SAME PATIENT *(Five minutes later)*: Hello, Doc. Glad to see you. See you again next year. *(He goes.)*

NEW NURSE: Who was that?

DENTIST: That was Mr. Jones. He sees me twice a year.

BE TRUE TO YOUR TEETH
OR THEY WILL BE FALSE TO YOU

16. SPORTS & GAMES

WEIGHTLIFTER: I can lift an elephant with one hand.

ROGER: I don't believe you.

WEIGHTLIFTER: Okay, bring me an elephant with one hand and I'll prove it.

Did you hear about the football player who asked his coach to flood the field? He wanted to go in as a sub.

A little boy knocked on the door of a friend's house. When the friend's mother answered, he said, "Can Leonard come out and play?"

"I'm afraid not," said Leonard's mother. "It's too wet and Leonard has a cold."

"Well, then," said the little boy, "can his football come out and play?"

SAL: Did you hear about the Teacher-Student football game?

HAL: Who won?

SAL: No one. The teachers were so mean, they refused to pass the ball.

PIT: I met someone who is so dumb, he thinks a football coach has four wheels.

PAT: How many wheels *does* it have?

COACH: Elmer, you can be the end, guard, and tackle.

ELMER: That's great, coach!

COACH: Yes, sit at the end of the bench, guard the water bucket, and tackle anyone who gets near it.

WORLD'S BEST TALKING DOG JOKE

Walking down the street, a man was stopped by someone who wanted to sell a talking dog for ten dollars.

The man couldn't believe his ears when the dog said, "Please buy me. I'm a great dog. I played professional football. I was even nominated most valuable player."

"That dog really does talk!" the man gasped. "Why in the world do you want to sell him for only ten dollars?"

"He never played professional football," said the dog's owner, "and I can't stand liars."

WORLD'S STUPIDEST FOOTBALL JOKE

"Okay, Smith," said the coach, "get in there and tackle 'em!"

Smith went into the game. Soon the opposing team was doubled over with laughter. The game had to be stopped.

"What are you doing?" asked the coach. "Why aren't you tackling the other team?"

"Oh–tackle!" said Smith. "I thought you said tickle."

MOTHER MONSTER: Why don't you play football with your little brother?
LITTLE MONSTER: Aw, Mom. I'd much rather have a real football to kick around.

What do you call a 300-pound football player with a short temper?
"Sir."

FATHER: Well, Son, did you make the school football team?
SON: I'm not sure, Dad. The coach took one look at me and said, "This is the end."

NUT: Are you a Giant fan?
TUT: Yes.
NUT: Well, I'm a little air conditioner myself.

DON: Did you hear about the karate
    expert who joined the army?
JOHN: No, what happened to him?
DON: The first time he saluted, he nearly
    killed himself.

GUS: Did you hear about the big fight at
the bus station?
RUSS: No, what happened?
GUS: Two tickets got punched.

Did you hear the joke about the boxing
glove? It'll knock you out.

BOXER: Feel my muscles. They're like
potatoes.
TRAINER: Yes, mashed potatoes.

NAN: Did you hear about the mean
wrestler who was pretty and ugly
at the same time?
DAN: How could that be?
NAN: Well, he was pretty ugly.

LES: My watch says it's eight-ish.
BESS: Mine says it's nine-ish.
JESS: Ten-ish, anyone?

FLO: Where are you taking that skunk?
JOE: To the gym.
FLO: What about the smell?
JOE: Oh, he'll get used to it.

ROCK: You must be a great bowler.
JOCK: How did you know?
ROCK: I can tell by your pin head.

RAY: You can't be a good bowler.
BONG: Why do you say that?
BING: Your mind is always in the gutter.

"Are you ready out there in radio land for your morning exercises? Good. Now—up, down, up, down, up, down. Now the other eyelid.

YOU: I bet I can jump across the street.
(When your friend says that you can't, walk across the street and jump.)

FLIP: I know a dancer who can lift her leg over her head.
FLOP: That's nothing. I know a sailor who can sit on his chest.

COACH: What this team needs is life!
MANAGER: Aw, coach, don't you think thirty days is enough?

The teacher asked the class to write a composition about baseball. One minute later, Henry turned in his paper. It read, "Game called on account of rain."

LITTLE LEAGUE CATCHER: Can I take time out to clean my mask?
COACH: What happened?
LITTLE LEAGUE CATCHER: My bubble gum popped.

What do you call a dog that stands behind home plate.
The catcher's mutt.

Who is the vampire's favorite person on the baseball team?
The bat boy.

THE WORLD'S SILLIEST BASEBALL JOKE

A professional baseball player was walking along the street one day when, to his horror, he saw a baby about to fall from a window. He dashed to the building and caught the baby, who was saved – unhurt. However, the force of habit proved too much for him. Without realizing what he was doing, he straightened up and threw the baby to first base.

Why did Cinderella lose the game for her team?

She ran away from the ball.

DUSTY: Mom, I can't find my baseball glove.
MOTHER: Did you look in the car?
DUSTY: Where in the car?
MOTHER: Try the glove compartment.

SHOPPER *(in sports shop)*: May I have a baseball glove for my son?
CLERK: Sorry, madam, we don't swap.

CHILD *(at first baseball game)*: Daddy, why is that man running?
FATHER: Because he hit the ball.
CHILD: Is he afraid it's going to hit him back?

LITTLE WILLIE *(looking at a catcher's mask)*: Why do they make that man wear a mask?
LITTLE LILY: Maybe it keeps him from biting the other players.

Did you hear about the baseball team that was so rich, all its bases were loaded?

The teacher was giving her first grade class a quiz on counting. Carol got things started by counting to ten.

"Now, Albert," said the teacher, "you take over by beginning with 11."

"11, 14, 23, 42, 36," said Albert.

"What kind of counting is that?" asked the teacher.

"Who's counting?" replied Albert. "I'm calling signals."

RITCHIE *(at baseball game)*: Can I give money to that man who's crying?
FATHER: That's very kind of you, son. What's he crying about?
RITCHIE: "Hot dogs! Peanuts! Popcorn!"

STANLEY: We played baseball in school today and I stole second base.
MOTHER: Well, you march right over to school and give it back.

BASEBALL JOKES YOU'LL NEVER WANT TO HEAR

"Did you hear the joke about the fast pitch?"

"Never mind, you just missed it."

"Did you hear the joke about the pop fly?"

"Never mind. It's way over your head."

"Did you hear the joke about your pitching style?"

"Never mind. It's foul."

LOU: A new pitcher is coming into the ball
    game.
PRU: That's a relief!

SAM: I have a chance for the soccer team.
PAM: I didn't know they were raffling it
    off.

TIMMY: Did you hear about the soccer
    player who didn't do well in school?
JIMMY: No.
TIMMY: He was a left back.

In ancient Greece the gods challenged the
mortals to a game of soccer. The gods
were surprised to see that one of the
members of the mortals' team was half
man and half horse.

"Who on earth is that?" asked Zeus.

"That," said the mortals' captain, "is our
centaur forward."

Why did the weightlifter wear black suspenders?
To keep his shoulders down.

What goes putt, putt, putt, putt, putt?
A bad golfer.

Why did the golfer wear two pairs of pants?
In case he got a hole in one.

"Daddy," said little Lucy, who was accompanying her father in a round of golf, "why mustn't the ball go into the little hole?"

Why are golf balls small and white?
Because if they were big and grey, they'd be elephants.

How do you make a golf ball float?
Take two scoops of ice cream, add root beer, then drop in the golf ball.

Why is it so hard to drive a golf ball?
Because it doesn't have a steering wheel.

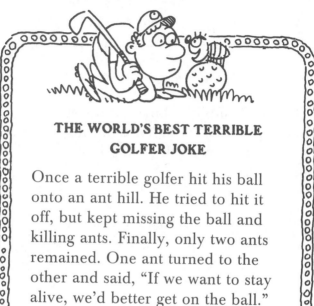

THE WORLD'S BEST TERRIBLE GOLFER JOKE

Once a terrible golfer hit his ball onto an ant hill. He tried to hit it off, but kept missing the ball and killing ants. Finally, only two ants remained. One ant turned to the other and said, "If we want to stay alive, we'd better get on the ball."

Where do caddies go to dance?
To the golf ball.

GEORGIE: I wish I had the money to buy a
million golf balls.
PORGIE: What would you do with a
million golf balls?
GEORGIE: Nothing. I just want the money.

The golfer took two enthusiastic swings at
the ball and missed both times. He looked
up at his companion and said, "That's
funny – this course is two inches lower
than the one I usually play."

At breakfast on Sunday, Oscar suddenly
announced that he had to go to the office.

"Listen," said Felix, "don't think you can
run off and play golf today and leave me
here with all the chores."

"Golf!" protested Oscar, grabbing a
piece of toast. "Golf is the furthest thing
from my mind. Pass the putter!"

NED: Lost your job as a caddy?
TED: Yes, I could do the work all right, but I just couldn't learn not to laugh.

Tom and Jerry were playing golf when a bird flew overhead.

"Look at that duck." Tom said.

"That's not a duck," said Jerry. "That's a goose."

"Duck!"

"Goose!"

And so the argument went. A golfer behind them, playing the hole, yelled, "Fore!" and hit the ball.

Tom saw the ball coming and shouted, "Duck!"

Jerry shouted back, "Goose!"

B-O-I-N-G!

What does a dog use for playing golf?
    A kennel club.

When do boxers start wearing gloves?
When it gets cold.

SALLY: What's the difference between a basketball, a boxing glove, and a bottle of glue?
ALLY: I don't know.
SALLY: A basketball if round, and a boxing glove isn't.
ALLY: But what about the glue?
SALLY: That's where you get stuck.

FRED: What do you call a blond stick used in billiards?
RED: Tan cue?
FRED: You're welcome!

17. NO MORE MISTER NICE GUY!

"Our dog is just like one of the family."
   "Which one?"

"This place isn't fit for a dog."
   "Yes, it is—come right in."

"I just came from the beauty parlor."
   "What's the matter—weren't they open?"

"Some people grow up and spread cheer.
You just grew up and spread."

"What kind of idiot do you think I am?"
  "I don't know. What other kinds are there?"

"I have an idea."
  "Your luck is improving."

"What you lack in intelligence you make up for in stupidity."

"It takes all kinds of people to make up this world—too bad you're not one of them."

"I'm not myself today."
  "I noticed the improvement right away."

"I didn't come here to be insulted."
  "Oh? Where do you usually go?"

"I'd like to find a hat to match my eyes."
"Sorry, we don't carry bloodshot hats."

"I earn a living by my wits."

"Well, half a living is better than none."

"What nice hands you have."

"My hands are soft, because I wear gloves at night."

"And do you also sleep with your hat on?"

"You are living proof that wisdom doesn't come with age."

"Someone once told me always to be myself."

"Well, you couldn't have gotten worse advice."

JOEY: People say you're so conceited you write letters to yourself.
ZOEY: Dear me . . .
JOEY: Yes, that's how they begin.

"What time is it?"
  "Sorry, but my watch is on the bum."
  "I know that—but what time is it?"

PROUD FATHER: My baby is the spitting image of me.
NEIGHBOR: What do you care, as long as it's healthy?

"My fiance says I'm the prettiest and most interesting girl he's ever met."

"And you'll trust yourself for life to a liar like that?"

"Whenever I'm in the dumps, I buy new clothes."

"So—that's where you get them!"

"Your face reminds me of a movie star—Lassie."

"Do you think I'm a fool?"

"No, but what's my opinion against thousands of others?"

"When is feeding time at the zoo?"

"One o'clock. If you hurry, you can still get a bite."

"I can trace my ancestors all the way back to royalty."

"King Kong?"

"I'm a bookworm."

"Oh, I thought you were just the ordinary kind."

"You're so stupid, if you shot an arrow into the air, you'd miss."

"Did I ever show you this picture? It's my father holding me on his knee when I was a baby."

"I see. He was a ventriloquist."

"I have a hunch."

"Really? And I thought you were just round-shouldered."

HUCK: Did the mudpack help your wife's appearance?

CHUCK: It did for a few days, but then it fell off.

"I heard you were at the dog show the other day."

"Yes, I was."

"Win any prizes?"

"My great-grandfather fought with General Lee; my grandfather fought with the British, and my father fought with the Americans."

"Your family can't get along with anybody, can they?"

"When you were born, you were so ugly that the doctor slapped your mother."

"There are hundreds of ways of making money, but only one honest way."

"What's that?"

"Aha! I knew you wouldn't know."

"What's the idea of telling everyone that I'm stupid?"

"Sorry, I didn't realize it was a secret."

"My mind seems to wander lately."

"Don't worry. It's too weak to go very far."

WANT AD

Man to work as garbage collector.
Good salary and all you can eat.

"What, in your opinion, do you consider
the height of stupidity?"

"How tall are you?"

Zeke, owner of the general store, was the
meanest, most insulting man in town.

One day a man walked into a store with
a duck under his arm.

"Say, what are you doing with that pig?"
said Zeke.

"Are you crazy?" the man replied.
"Can't you see that this is a duck—not a
pig?"

"I wasn't talking to you," Zeke sneered.
"I was talking to the duck."

IGOR: Commissar! Commissar! The troops are revolting!

COMMISSAR: Well, you're pretty revolting yourself.

"Want to lose ten pounds of ugly fat?"

"Sure."

"Cut off your head."

"Will this ointment make me smart?"

"No, this is ordinary medicine, not a miracle drug."

"He's played his last practical joke."

"How so?"

"Just before he died, he left his brain to science."

"You've got a very large stomach."

"Do you think I should diet?"

"Oh, the color's all right—it's just the size."

"You shouldn't make fun of my looks. All human beings are made in the same mold."

"Yes, but some are moldier than others."

"You have a very striking face. It should be struck more often."

CUSTOMER *(in clothing store)*: Have you any ties to match my eyes?

CLERK: No, but we have soft hats to match your head.

"I'm speechless!"
  "If only you'd stay that way!"

"I heard about your wit."
  "Oh, it's nothing."
  "Yes, that's what I heard."

"I thought my razor was dull until I heard you talk."

"If you were my husband, I'd feed you poison."
  "If I were your husband, I'd take it."

"You think you're a big cheese—but you only smell like one."

The last time I saw a mouth like yours, it had a fishhook in it."

"The more I think of you, the less I think of you."

TIP: My doctor advised me to exercise
  with dumbbells.
TOP: So?
TIP: Care to join me in the gym?

"Where do all the bugs go in winter?"
  "Search me."
  "No, thanks, I just wanted to know."

"You're half an hour late. I've been
standing here like a fool."
  "I can't help how you stand."

"I've seen more interesting faces on
clocks."

"Whatever is eating you must be suffering
from indigestion."

"You have an even disposition—always
rotten."

"When I get old and ugly, will you still talk to me?"

"Don't I?"

"Do you like my company?"

"I don't know. What company are you with?"

"I'll be seeing you."

"Not if I see you first."

18. GOING CRAZY

BYSTANDER *(helping up victim who slipped on the ice)*: It's a lucky thing for you that this accident happened in front of a doctor's house.

VICTIM: Not really–I'm the doctor.

I know a woman who is so lazy, when she broke her leg, her bones refused to knit.

NIP: How did you break your leg?
TUCK: See that hole over there?
NIP: Yes.
TUCK: Well, I didn't.

MOTHER *(scolding child)*: If you fall from that tree and break both your legs, don't you come running to me!

DOCTOR: You have a broken leg, a broken arm, four fractured ribs, and probably a brain concussion. Are you in great pain?
PATIENT: Only when I laugh!

DOCTOR: What happened to your thumb?
PATIENT: I hit the wrong nail.

VISITOR: My friend was run over by a steamroller and he's in this hospital. What room is he in?

NURSE: Room 105, 106, 107, and 108.

PATIENT: Doctor, doctor, I feel like a sheep!

DOCTOR: That's baaa-d.

Lem and Clem were walking along the railroad tracks. Lem saw a man's leg. "I think that's Joe's leg," he said.

Then they saw a body. "I think that's Joe's body," said Clem.

Walking on, they came to a head. Lem picked it up and started shaking it.

"Hey, Joe!" he said in a worried voice. "Joe–are you hurt?"

A city dude went to a ranch to buy a horse. He saw a beautiful pony and asked what kind it was. "That's a palomino," the rancher said.

"Well," the city dude thought for a minute. "Any friend of yours is a friend of mine."

PATIENT: Doctor, doctor, I keep thinking
    I'm invisible!
DOCTOR: Who said that?

PRISONER *(to judge)*: What floor are we on, Your Honor?

JUDGE: The second floor.

PRISONER: I'm going upstairs.

JUDGE: What for?

PRISONER: I want to take my case to a higher court.

JUDGE: The next person who raises his voice in this court will be thrown out.

PRISONER: Hip, hip, hooray! Hip, hip, hooray!

SCHOOLTEACHER *(visiting the jail)*: What are you doing?

PRISONER: I'm sawing the bars.

SCHOOLTEACHER: Tut, tut, where's your grammar? You should say, "I'm seeing the bars!"

A prisoner escaped from jail and said to a little boy he met, "Hooray! I'm free! I'm free!"

"So what?" replied the little boy. "I'm four!"

JUDGE: Order! Order in the court!
DEFENDANT: I'll have a hamburger on a
roll with mustard and a Coke, please.

GIL: I'm going to bring my pet bird to school.

WILL: What kind of bird is it?

GIL: A keet.

WILL: Don't you mean a parakeet?

GIL: No, I only have one.

KIM: You remind me of a school closed for vacation.

DIM: How is that?

KIM: You have no class.

The telephone rang in the office of the school principal. "Hello, may I speak to the principal, please?"

"This is the principal."

"I'm calling to say that my son cannot come to school today because he has a bad cold."

"Who is this speaking, please?"

"This is my father."

Did you hear about the man who was so absent-minded he poured ketchup on his shoelaces and tied knots in his spaghetti?

FLIES FOR LUNCH

CAL: There's a fly in this ice cream.
SCHOOL COOK: Serves him right. Let him freeze.

SAL: There's a fly in this butter.
SCHOOL COOK: No, there isn't.
SAL: Look for yourself.
SCHOOL COOK: First of all, it's not a fly, it's a moth. Second, it isn't butter, it's margarine.

HAL: There's a moth in my soup!
SCHOOL COOK: That's right. The fly is on vacation.

SCHOOL COOK: I put some extra pepper in the chili. Was it too hot?

MICHAEL: Why, no, smoke always comes out of my ears.

MARCO: Our school cook is terrible.

POLO: How bad is he?

MARCO: He's so bad, we pray after we eat.

DINAH: The crust on that apple pie was tough.

SCHOOL COOK: That wasn't the crust. That was the paper plate.

ALLAN: Why is this bread full of holes?

SCHOOL COOK: It's whole (hole) wheat bread.

SCHOOL COOK: Eat your vegetables. Green things are good for you.

RITA: Okay, I'll have some pistachio ice cream.

"My, but the flies are thick around here."
   "Well, you're not so bright yourself."

Sign in school cafeteria:

> **DO NOT CRUMBLE YOUR BREAD**
> **OR ROLL IN YOUR SOUP**

DONNA: I understand that fish is brain food.

DON: Yes, I eat it all the time.

DONNA: Oh, well, there goes another scientific theory.

When an executioner checked in at a hotel, the clerk asked him what kind of room he wanted. "A small one," he replied. "I just need a place to hang my hat and a few friends."

What did the
beaver say to the
tree?

"It's been nice
gnawing you!"

What did one
caveman say to
the other
caveman?

"BC'ing you!"

INDEX

347

348

349